NINE YEARS IN THE SADDLE

WRITTEN BY

JAMES V. LEE

Printed in the United States of America
First Edition, 1998
Revised Edition, 1999

ISBN: 0-9663870-0-7
Library of Congress Catalog Card Number: 99-94006

Salado Press
P.O. Box 719
Salado, Texas 76571

ACKNOWLEDGMENTS

I wish to thank the following people for their assistance, encouragement, and support throughout this project:

Judson Warren (Dud) Lee, my father
Mary Westmoreland Lee, Dud's wife
Hazel Juanita Lee, my wife
Gail Lee Dunson, my daughter
Lilla Bessonette Barnes, my friend
Jeanne McCarty Moran, my friend

I also wish to thank the following for their assistance in helping me locate my father:

Doris Greenlee White, my aunt
Lucille Simpson, my friend
Howard Wright, my cousin
Colita Lee Schalbar, my aunt

JAMES V. LEE

TABLE OF CONTENTS

PROLOGUE

The twin-engine plane had delivered me to a small air terminal at Springfield, Missouri, which was nearly empty. As I entered the terminal, I heard a woman whom I had never met before exclaim,

"Here he is! I found him!"

She led me to a waiting television crew, which began to film this historic meeting between me and the elderly gentleman who accompanied her.

Dressed in western attire from his wide-brimmed hat to his cowboy boots, his six-foot frame retained a certain vigor that belied his years. When he saw me, a smile spread across his square face illuminated by alert, penetrating blue eyes as he extended a firm hand, molded by a lifetime of hard work.

While the camera rolled, the interviewer plied us with questions about my search that culminated in this meeting. This is a story of a man whom I never got to know until he was eighty-one-years-old, my father.

JAMES V. LEE

CHAPTER 1
THE MAKING OF A COWBOY

I guess it all started when I was a kid. Very early, life introduced me to such ideas as resourcefulness, self-reliance, and gumption, the very qualities vital to survival on a big ranch where I sometimes saw no other person for weeks at a time. But except for the low pay, punching cattle was the best job I ever had.

When I was born on September 11, 1907, they named me Judson Warren Brown Lee. Later, I dropped the name Brown, and my dad wanted to call me Dud from the beginning. Nobody else liked that name, but it didn't make any difference to Dad, so I have gone by the name of Dud nearly all my life. He also gave peculiar names to two of my sisters.

At that time, Dad was working a little hillside farm belonging to my grandfather about fifteen miles south of Brownwood, Texas. The second child in the family, I was born in a two-room house about a year-and-a-half after my brother Lyo. Then Dad became a deputy sheriff at Brady, Texas, where we lived in the courthouse. When I was two-and-a-half years old, my mother Effie Wright Lee died when she gave birth to my brother Bud, and I went to live with Grandpa and Grandma Wright. My dad left at that time, so I have almost no recollection of my parents at an early age. The Wrights had a son named Reuben who was five months older than I. Two of his younger sisters Leesie and Alta were near our age, so we all kind of grew up together.

I also spent some time with Grandfather and Grandmother Lee. He was a Baptist preacher and we went to church in a wagon every Sunday night. The church was about three miles from where we lived. Quilts padded the wagon bed so we could sleep if we wanted to. Usually, we just hung our feet off the back end.

Often we sang because all of my uncles and aunts were good singers and played various instruments. I just went back and forth between grandparents until I was age seven.

At that time I was living with the Lees and started to school, but I didn't go but for a short time because my dad showed up, and I went with him. He had married my stepmother, who would eventually present me with three half sisters—Colita, Doris, and Coiness—and one half brother Elwin. My stepmother had some unremarkable qualities. I'll just let it go by saying I never got along with her.

At this time, we lived on the Colorado River near Winchell, Texas, where Dad taught me and Lyo how to swim. He had a simple technique. He just threw us into the water. I was trying to get back to the bank, but couldn't keep my head out of the water, nor could I touch bottom. I finally got out of the river by ducking my head and pushing off the bottom. That gave me the idea that if I put my face under the water, I could swim. After that, whenever I started to sink, I would just put my face under water as far as I could and start swimming. Both Lyo and I got to be good swimmers. Dad also had an old boat on the river, and we fished a lot.

Since there was no water at the house for the horses, Lyo and I used to ride the horses down to the river to water them. This was about my first experience at riding horses. We stayed on that farm for two years.

Then some guy talked Dad into moving to Oklahoma. We moved in a covered wagon, going through the Dallas, Ft. Worth area to Checotah, Oklahoma. Dad tried to farm that year, but he never had any luck at farming. Everywhere he went to farm, something always happened, or he had bad luck. He just couldn't make it as a farmer. We stayed in Oklahoma that year, and everybody got sick except me. All had chills and fever. There were two or three families that lived close by that also got sick and had to go to bed. Nearby was a little town called Texana with nothing but a post office and store where they sent me to buy medicine for everybody. I had a little bay mare that I rode bareback. I guess everybody had charge accounts, because I didn't take any money.

I got some schooling in Oklahoma. I was in the first grade, and Lyo and I sat together at a double desk. I was always clowning around and getting into trouble. The teacher would whack me over the head with a ruler, a big pencil, or whatever he had in his hand. He was a mean teacher. One time when I was acting like a baby, getting all the kids to laugh and just having a ball, the teacher called me up front. I thought I was going to get a whipping, and bravely swaggered up there. I didn't mind much for a whipping. It didn't hurt that badly and it made me feel big. But the teacher pulled up a straight chair, sat down, and put me on his knee. He sang lullabies to me for ten minutes. When he put me down, I dropped my head, slunk back to my seat, and never did that again.

In Oklahoma, I got acquainted with wild

strawberries, dewberries, and blackberries, which seemed to grow everywhere in that part of the country. Pecan trees lined the creek. Even with all this natural stuff, Dad decided to move back to my grandpa's old farm and try farming one more year. By now I was eight years old and tried to help Dad raise cotton. But the weather was dry and the cotton never did get very big; consequently, the harvest was poor. In September of that year, my stepmother gave birth to Colita in the same house where I was born.

Right after Colita was born, Dad took a train for Bisbee, Arizona. After he acquired a house, he sent for the rest of the family. He had gone to work in the copper mines there.

This is where I got my first taste of the mountains, which were gravelly and steep. We were afraid to climb too far because if you ever started sliding, there was nothing to stop you but the bottom. No grass, brush, nor trees grew on the mountain. I guess there was too much mineral in it for anything to grow. We lived right at the foot of a hill and the highway came right by our house. This is where I got my first treats. Dad bought a box of apples and told us to help ourselves. The only time I had fruit previously was at Christmas when I got an apple, an orange, and maybe a few nuts, no presents. Well, one time Dad did give me a pocketknife and I thought it was one of the greatest things I had ever received. That knife gave me a glimpse into some of my future relationship with Lyo. I don't remember what he got, but he wanted my knife. We went out to a haystack by the barn, and he wanted to show me how he could throw that knife over the haystack. Well, he threw it into the hay somewhere, and we never did find it. But the main thing he wanted to do was get rid of that knife because he couldn't have it. That caused a lot of conflict between us, but I didn't say anything about it because I knew we would both get a whipping.

We stayed in Bisbee three years where I got the best schooling I ever received. I went to school the year round with a week off every three months. Later, when I went back to Texas schools, I was way ahead of my class.

We left Bisbee when I was twelve. Dad decided there was a place in Texas where he, with the help of his three boys, could get rich picking cotton. The crops were good and wages were up.

I did well at picking cotton because I applied myself as I did at any work I was supposed to do. But Lyo hated picking cotton. He hated everything about a farm and wouldn't work at it. After a month, it started raining and continued all fall. Much of the cotton was ruined. We never had more than two or three days of sunshine at a time. When the rain did stop, the dew would be so heavy in the morning that you couldn't pick until sometime after noon when the sun dried off the cotton. Then we would work until dark and hope for a dry day tomorrow.

After this, Dad rented a farm from an old guy east of Brooksmith, Texas, next to a railroad. He had a lot of oats to thrash, which provided Lyo and me with the first job we ever got paid for. When we weren't in school, we thrashed oats and put them into boxcars. The oats were loaded through a door in the middle of the boxcar, and we had to take big scoops and shovel the oats to each end of the car. As the boxcar filled up, we put boards over the door, working from the bottom up. Finally, the boxcar would fill up, and we had to crawl out a hole in top of the boxcar. With all that dust and oat husks sticking to our sweaty bodies, our skin would be stinging and burning by the time we finished the job. About a quarter of a mile away was a creek where we would go and dive in with our clothes on.

Then this old fellow Dad worked with lost his mind. I was with him the night he went completely off his rocker. He wanted to go everywhere and wanted me to go with him. He wanted me to get his horse and buggy. He didn't have a horse and buggy. He insisted that there were horses in the pasture and the buggy was in the barn. I couldn't handle him. Our house was about a quarter of mile from his, so I went home and told Dad what was happening. He took the old fellow to the hospital where he soon died. I never did know just what was wrong with him.

While we were at this place, Dad bought two horses and gave one to Lyo and the other one to me. Lyo wanted my horse, but I wouldn't trade. One cold morning the two of us went out in the field to catch the horses and ride them. Lyo grabbed my horse. I said,

"No, you can't have my horse. He's mine. You get your own horse."

We were arguing and shoving and pushing each other around. Lyo and I fought a lot anyway. I was about as big as he was from the time I was six years old. He wasn't going to let me have my horse, so he picked up a rock about the size of baseball and hit me right on the jaw. It knocked me out cold. He thought he had killed me. Badly scared, he just ran off instead of going to the house and telling anyone. When I woke up, I saw him down at the end of the field going into some brush. At this time, my stepmother's father, who was an old Civil War soldier, was staying with us. He had an old over-and-under rifle. The bottom barrel was a shotgun, the top barrel a .30 .30 caliber. I got the gun, loaded both barrels, and set out to look for Lyo. I meant to kill him. I chased him all day long through the woods, but never did get a shot at him. He would either be running or hiding behind a tree or in the brush. About sundown, I came home and put up the gun. A little later, when it was dark, Lyo sneaked back into the house. I didn't say anything to him. Funny, I had walked so much that day that I had kind of gotten over my mad spell. I didn't get to ride my horse, anyway.

The three of us boys started back to school at a little place near Brooksmith. I was so far ahead of the Texas schools that I skipped the fifth grade. I had already covered that material in Arizona.

But then, some time that fall, a strange thing happened. We came home from school one day, and there was absolutely nothing in the house. Nothing! No people, no furniture, no food. Nothing! Although we didn't know it, my dad and stepmother had separated. We decided to walk to Grandpa Lee's place.

We lived six miles from Brooksmith, and he lived six miles in the other direction, about twelve miles by way of the road. We shaved three miles by cutting across the country. When we told him what had happened, he let us stay with him. Shortly after that, Lyo moved out and went to work for a farmer nearby who needed a hand. I worked for Grandpa about a month, until one day a guy came riding up on a big chestnut sorrel stud horse. This man had part of the Bale outfit, a big ranch that covered a lot of country. He raised sheep, goats, cows, and horses and was looking for somebody to help him, since it was about time for the sheep to start lambing. He not only was good to work for, but he also sent me to school.

This man appeared to be about forty-five years of age but was married to a fourteen-year-old girl. Any time I was around the house, she told me tales about her husband and how they got together, none of which was interesting to me. She wasn't much older than I was, but I wasn't thinking about girls at that age.

I worked for this man all that year and the next summer, handling cattle, goats, and sheep. I hated sheep because they didn't have brains enough to stay out of the cold. Some of the ewes wouldn't claim their lambs, so we marked the lambs with paint and matched them to the mama ewes, which we also marked. Every morning and every night we had to gather up twenty or more lambs and put them with their mothers and hold them until they started nursing.

Then we had some goats that were a nuisance. One was an old buck that stayed in a six-acre pen stretching from the barn to the creek. This fellow had given me a saddle that was all in pieces. I had some leather strings and was trying to tie it all together and get it in shape so I could ride on it to gather up some cattle. Punching cows was what I really wanted to do. While I was working on this saddle next to the barn, the danged goat let out a big baaah. I didn't even look around. I just was squatting down and working on my saddle. Suddenly this goat butted me from behind and knocked me plumb over the saddle. Then he just ran off toward the creek hollering baaah. If I had had a gun, I would have shot a goat, and we would have had barbecued cabrito.

In August of that year, I decided to hunt for Dad. Although I had no idea where he went, I knew he used to be a deputy sheriff in Brady. Bud was at Grandpa Lee's. I went over there and told Grandpa that I would like to take Bud and go to Brady to look for Dad. He agreed and drove us in a buggy to Brooksmith where I bought some clothes for both of us before boarding a train for Brady.

When we stepped off the train at Brady, the first person I saw was Dad. He was coming along beside the train driving a jitney which are called taxis now. Jitney drivers met the train and took people to the hotels or wherever they needed to go. Dad picked up Bud and me and took us home. He and my stepmother were back together. Lyo had a job washing dishes. Bud couldn't get a job, being only nine years old, but I got a job in a broom factory, which played out about the same time Lyo's job played out. So Lyo said to me,

"Whadda you say we go to San Antone?"

"That's O.K. with me," I replied.

We headed down the road to San Antonio with just the clothes we had on. We didn't have any ideas as to what this old world was about. After we got down the road a little way, a salesman, known as a drummer in those days, picked us up. He was in his mid-twenties and entertained us by teaching us dog Latin. As we neared San Antonio, he said,

"Well fellows, I'm sorry, but I'm not going any farther. I've got to turn off here, so I'll let y'all out."

Well, we didn't go on to San Antone. We took another road and started back home. As we walked, we talked dog Latin all the time to kind of break up the monotony. When we got hungry, we went to some farmer's house and begged them out of a sandwich or something other to eat. Of course, we could get water nearly anywhere from windmills or wells along the road. It took us four days to get back, and we walked the entire distance. Coming home was really strange. I talked to Lyo about it years later, and he didn't understand any more than I did. When we got home, nobody said, "Where have you been?" "What have you been doing?" "How long have you been gone?"

Nothing. They acted like we stepped out thirty minutes before and just walked back in.

But Dad and Lyo weren't getting along together too well.

That's why Lyo decided to leave home. As he walked across the pasture, I was pretty broken hearted because, in spite of all our little spats, I needed Lyo. He was kind of a brace to me. I needed somebody to relate to and somebody to depend upon. He was older than I was, and I took him to be the boss. He didn't stay gone long, but returned and went to work. I had another job too. I asked him one day,

"How come we don't go to school?"

"I don't know. Nobody ever said anything about it, and I don't care whether or not I go to school."

"Well, I'm not too crazy about going to school either, but I just wondered why we didn't go."

We seldom saw Dad. I know he did something besides drive that jitney. A few days later, Lyo asked,

"Do you know where Grandpa Wright lives?"

"Well, no. Not really."

"I do. He lives somewhere around San Saba, Richland Springs, I think. Whadda you say we go down there?"

We were both out of anything to do, so we took off walking. The weather wasn't too bad when we left Brady, but the second day, it turned cold and the wind blew hard. It got bad before we got to Richland Springs on a Saturday evening. We were walking down the street and I said,

"I don't know where Grandpa lives. Do you?"

"No, but we'll ask somebody here where he is."

Lyo addressed a big tall guy coming down the street, "Say mister, do you know W. B. Wright?"

The man eyed him a little bit and responded,

"Yeah. I do. Who are you?"

"W. B. Wright is my grandfather."

"Oh, yeah, yeah, I'm Elmer, W. B. Wright's son."

I spoke up, "Oh, I remember you, but it has been a long time since I saw you. I was a little bitty kid when I saw you last."

"Well, I'm going over to see Dad tomorrow."

"That's where we want to go," I said.

"I'm leaving town in a few minutes. Just get into the wagon and you can go with me."

We stayed all night with Elmer. After breakfast the next day, he took us to Grandpa Wright's house.

Lyo went to work for Grandpa, but I went to school along with Reuben. They bought me the first new suit of clothes I ever had. In those days, everybody my age wore knee pants. They also bought me new shoes and ties. I was very happy to stay there. Reuben and I goofed off a lot, fishing and hunting. We didn't do much work. But Grandpa would say,

"Reuben, I want you boys to do so and so today."

And as soon as we finished breakfast, we'd grab an extra biscuit and piece of meat from the table, stick it in our pockets, leave, and not come back until sundown. But we did all the chores. Grandpa didn't have to do anything. We fed all the horses and cows. We milked the cows before breakfast and again before night. But whatever Grandpa wanted done during the day just had to go because we weren't there.

Grandpa had a big orchard full of apple, pear, peach, and plum trees. He also had grapes by the bunches, all kinds of red ones and white ones which we tried to eat as fast as they got ripe.

Reuben taught me to use a slingshot now. We carried them around our necks at all times and became expert shots with them. We could knock the eye out of a rabbit.

Sometimes we would kill a bird and then take turns holding it between our fingers while the other one shot it out of the hand from about thirty feet away. We often went out into the woods to kill a rabbit or bird and then roast it and eat it. Or if we found somebody's chicken out in the woods, we would shoot it and eat it. Whatever was left over we used for fish bait.

Grandpa had a big pond about twenty feet deep in the middle, which supplied water for the house. It had some big fish in it, but we didn't know it. We just knew that it had a lot of perch, which really weren't fit to eat because they were so small. But one day I baited my hook with the guts from a dove and dropped it deep into the pond. Then I just stuck the pole into the bank while I fished for perch. All of a sudden, I saw that line go under. I grabbed the pole and reared back on it like I was going to throw the fish into the woods. But when I jerked it, the line broke next to the pole. I just stood there looking into the water, but I knew it was gone. Reuben said,

"Boy! That must have been a pretty big fish you were holding, or else it was a log."

I said, "That wasn't a log. It was alive! I could feel it!"

About that time, the cork on the line popped to the surface. I wasn't wearing anything but pants, so I jumped in and tried to grab the line. But the cork disappeared, and I got back out. After a couple of minutes, the cork popped up again. I jumped in again and waited for the cork to appear again. Suddenly, it bobbed up right under my nose. I grabbed it in my hand, flipped over on my back and started swimming to the bank. But the fish was jerking me as much as I was jerking him. Just before I got to the bank, the fish came off the hook, which he had completely straightened out.

Reuben and I excitedly told Grandpa what happened. So he got out his trotline to go back to the pond with us to try to land that fish. Lyo was at the house and we tried to get him to go with us. He just said,

"Nah, I ain't going out with you kids. I'm not going to waste my time that way."

He was acting a lot bigger because he was a year older than we were.

But he was wrong. Not long after Grandpa got his trotline in the water, we pulled out a sixteen-pound catfish. That excited Lyo. Then he wanted to go back and fish with us, but we had already had our fun for the day.

The next year, Dad rented the farm from Grandpa, and Lyo and I helped. We only stayed for one year because Dad and Grandpa didn't get along very well. I don't know what the matter was. Nobody ever told me anything about it. Grandpa could get along with anybody. He was one of the best natured men I ever knew, and I can't imagine anybody not getting along with him. Lyo and I didn't get anything for working for Dad that year, but he kind of saw to it that we had a little money to get by on from time-to-time.

Then Dad rented another farm the following year about six miles from Grandpa. So I went to the same school. Dad decided to raise watermelons, and he grew the largest melons I have ever seen. Some weighed eighty to ninety pounds and were at least two-and-a-half feet long. We took wagonloads of watermelons to Brownwood to sell. We gave watermelons to the neighbors. We fed watermelons to the hogs. And we ate watermelons until they were running out of our ears. Since Lyo and I weren't making any money, he was getting itchy to leave. And the only thing that kept me from leaving was Trades Day each week in Brownwood.

CHAPTER 2
MAN STUFF

Going to Brownwood to trade put a fair amount of common sense into my fifteen-year-old head. I always looked forward to Mondays when I could go there with Dad. Mostly, we traded horses and mules. Dad boosted my excitement by giving me a horse just to use for trading. This old horse had a sore on his back that wouldn't heal. And riding him after the sore scabbed over would just tear off the scab again. Other than that, he was a good horse and easy to ride. I traded him for a little paint horse, which I rode for a while right after I got him. I didn't like him much because he was lazy and walked with his head down. No rider cuts a good figure on a horse with his head down, so I traded him off for a stout little sorrel which was about fifteen years old. Since he was so old, I traded him for two horses about a month later, one good one and one that wasn't worth a hoot. I sold both of them and just kept the money.

But I had a roan mare that Dad had given me the preceding spring, which I used for a saddle horse to go to dances and other places. Although she had a clubfoot, I didn't want to trade her.

At this time, Dad's youngest brother Frank wrote to Lyo from New Mexico and invited him to come out there. When Lyo went to New Mexico, he left behind a really pretty two-year-old sorrel horse named Mustard. Dad said he paid Lyo for the horse. Lyo said he didn't. I don't know who was right, but I doubt that Dad paid him anything for the horse. Anyway, I traded my roan mare to Dad for Lyo's sorrel horse and rode him that year and into the next spring. But the horse had a bad habit of stuffing himself with anything he could find to eat. When I fed him oats, I mixed in rocks to try to keep him from getting so much in his mouth at one time. But he would still get choked up. We had a ditch about six feet deep and six feet across, and every time the horse got choked, I jumped him back and forth across that ditch until he got his food down.

To fill in between Trade Days, I went to work for Rouse Harrell who lived about a mile from us. In the spring, I helped him clear off a lot of pasture for farming. For payment, he designated five acres for me, which I planted in cotton. Of course, I needed some money from time-to-time, so I asked Rouse,

"How do I go about getting some money? Could I borrow it from the bank?"

He said, "Yeah, just go to the banker and tell him what you've got. Tell them that you've got that sorrel horse, that you are working for me, and that you've got five acres of cotton that you will put up for collateral and borrow a hundred dollars."

As young as I was, the banker agreed to lend me the hundred dollars for the collateral. I bought a few clothes, but otherwise was pretty stingy with my money. I didn't spend it on anything that I didn't have to, and it lasted me all year. Since my five acres was virgin soil, I only harvested two bales. However, when I sold my first bale, the next thing I did was go to the bank and pay off my note. After I closed the deal, the banker said,

"Son, when you need some more money, why don't you come back and talk to us? We will try to deal with you."

I thanked him and felt pretty proud of myself to know that a banker considered me to be that responsible. But I never had an opportunity to borrow from him again because Dad wanted to move to West Texas near O'Donnell and wanted me to go with him.

We loaded as much of his stuff as we could into a wagon and had somebody ship the rest. Dad drove the wagon pulled by two big mules, while I rode a horse named Buster and drove all the extra horses and mules. We were on the road about ten days, camping out along the way. We must have covered the better part of three hundred miles. I really enjoyed the trip even though the fall scenery wasn't much to look at. From Central Texas to West Texas, the landform changes radically. Instead of hills and wooded areas with many streams, the part of West Texas that hadn't been plowed up was a flat prairie sprinkled with scrub mesquite trees and bear grass with few streams. To me, living out in the open spaces and herding horses on a long drive seemed like living in the old West.

When we stopped near Polk City one night, we found the gyp water was too bad to drink. Therefore, we dry camped that night. At a little store, Dad bought a few cans of pineapple to keep us from getting so thirsty. This was the first pineapple I had ever eaten, and compared to gyp water, it was like nectar from heaven. After that, whenever I was going off some place and needed to take a lunch, I bought a loaf of bread and a can of pineapple and made a meal out of it.

After we arrived on the plains, we settled in a little rural community called O.K., which was about five miles southwest of O'Donnell. Dad rented a 360-acre farm and asked Lyo to come back from New Mexico and help him farm. He set aside thirty acres for Lyo and me to plant in cotton for helping him that year.

Lyo also did some work for a neighbor named Troy who made whiskey on the side. Troy and Dad got along very well. No strangers to mischief, Lyo and I tried to find his whiskey, which he kept well hidden because these were prohibition years. One night, Troy dug a big hole out in the field when nobody was around and buried a barrel of whiskey there. The next day, Troy said to Lyo,

"There is a bare place out in the field where a row has been skipped. Go hook up a team and plow over it two or three times."

Since we knew that Troy made whiskey, we immediately suspected that he had buried some whiskey there. Then at night when everybody was asleep, we dug down until we found the bunghole in the barrel. Then we put a hose into the whiskey and sucked it up with our mouths, pinched off the bottom of the hose, and drained the contents of the hose into a fruit jar. We would steal about a half a gallon and then not get any more for a long time.

Stealing Troy's whiskey was just something adventurous to do. I really didn't care anything about drinking the whiskey. My dislike for it goes back to about age two when my dad made himself toddy early one morning. Thinking it wouldn't hurt me, he also gave me a little one, which I drank. At that time, Dad was deputy sheriff at Brady and left immediately to go look for some stolen mules. We had a colored cook who came in a few minutes later and made herself toddy and also gave one to me.

I drank that, and then about fifteen minutes later, my mother came in and fixed herself toddy. I was still around and in her way, so she gave me toddy, which I drank. Not long after, my dad came in from town to eat breakfast and decided to fix himself another toddy before he ate. Not knowing that I had had two more since he left, he gave me another one. Then they sat down to eat breakfast but couldn't find me. After looking all through the house, Dad found me leaning up against the back wall of the house drunker than a skunk. After that, I never did care too much for whiskey.

Eventually, we became afraid that Troy would miss the whiskey, so we started replacing each half-gallon of whiskey with a half gallon of water. We did that for quite a while, and if Troy ever suspected us of watering down his whiskey, he never said anything to us about it.

Troy's whiskey making spilled over into one of his mules. This particular mule was pretty wild and prone to break through fences. Troy's stack lot, where he kept bundles of feed for his live stock, lay adjacent to his corral where he kept this mule penned up. Well, Troy had run off a batch of corn whiskey and dumped a big pile of whiskey waste in his stack lot. His mule kicked through the fence and ate a big batch of the whiskey tailings. The next morning when Lyo went out to harness the mule and go to work, he took one look at the mule and hollered over to me,

"Come over here. I want to show you something."

When I showed up, he said,

"I just got this mule out of the stack lot, 'cause he was just laying down in there."

We could see where the mule had been eating that cornmeal mash. When we got him to stand up, he just staggered around. When he tried to run, he fell down. Finally, no matter what we did to him, he wouldn't even move. That mule just lay down and quit the world.

Troy had been gone during this time, but returned home about ten o'clock. Lyo hadn't gone to work because he needed four mules and one was too drunk to plow. When Troy saw the condition of his mule, he said,

"Just let him lay there and sober up, and we'll hook him up tomorrow."

That was the first and only drunk mule I ever saw in my whole life. We talked about it for a few days, and everybody got a good laugh out it.

In the spring and early summer, the weather conditions were just right for raising cotton. The cotton was knee high and loaded with squares and bolls. And we still had a good growing season ahead of us. Dad thought he was finally going to make it as a farmer. He was sure the crop would produce three hundred bales, maybe four hundred. He was going to be a rich man. Then on June 19, a hailstorm blew in. Hail the size of baseballs beat the cotton into the ground. When the storm was over, where there had once been pretty cotton, the ground was as bare as if it had been freshly disc plowed. The wind even blew the roof off the car shed, which had adobe walls, and then the hail demolished the walls. Remarkably, the car was not damaged. Dad was just sick. Strangely, the hail did not hit the thirty acres that belonged to Lyo and me. Weather that fickle may be peculiar to West Texas. Anyone who has ever farmed in West Texas knows of instances when one farmer will get a good rain, and a neighbor right across the turn row won't get any.

We replanted the entire 330 acres as fast as we could. Dad had to borrow money to buy the cottonseed. Once again, the ground had plenty of moisture, the weather was warm, and the new crop grew rapidly. Soon the stalks loaded up with squares and blooms, promising a bumper crop after all. Dad was really happy. Despite all his troubles, this time he was going to make it. But then the dang armyworms came in by the billions and started eating the crop. We worked day and night spraying arsenic on the cotton to try to kill the armyworms. But the poison wasn't very effective. We finally harvested about twenty bales of poor quality cotton, which wasn't nearly enough to get Dad out of debt. Since the thirty acres belonging to Lyo and me was older cotton, the armyworms did not infest it. We bought a little Star Roadster with part of our money from the crop and gave the rest to Dad. He was pretty blue about the whole situation. After the crop failure, everything just fell apart.

Not long afterward, I was at Elmer Wright's house when Dad came over and said,

"I want you to come go with me."

"O.K." I said, "Where are we going?"

"To Big Spring."

It was about sixty miles to Big Spring and the nearest railroad. Dad talked all the way to town, telling me about all of his troubles, about how hard he had tried to be a man, about how hard he had tried to succeed at something, and about how everything he had attempted turned sour. And he said he was sorry the way he had treated us boys. He said,

"I know that whatever you are, you made yourself. I had nothing to do with it."

But he was wrong because he did have a lot influence on us. He taught us the basics. He taught us to be men. He taught us to respect other people. He just taught us a lot of things that he didn't realize that he had taught us. But of course, he didn't teach us anything about the ways of the world or how to get by because he had never been able to get by himself. He had done a lot of hoboing and such stuff, everything except the right things, I guess. When he said goodbye at Big Spring he said,

"I don't know when I will see you again, if ever. But I will try to get in touch with you some day."

Following his instructions I went back to O'Donnell and left his car where his old lady could find it.

Lyo decided to go back to New Mexico, but I wasn't ready to leave. I thought a lot of a girl I had been going with and didn't want to give her up. The next January we got married and that's when thing began to rock in a different direction. I was eighteen and she was sixteen.

Rita, Dud, and James Lee, 1929,
Bisbee, Arizona

CHAPTER 3
FAMILY PROBLEMS

Right after we married, I talked to a farmer about working for him, and he offered me a pretty good deal. My wife Rita was staying at her folks, and I told Old Man Greenlee, her father, what the guy offered me.

"Well," he advised, "I'll give you a better deal than that. I'll give you ten acres of cotton down on the lower end of the place where I know it will make good cotton. And during the summer and harvest, I'll pay you thirty-five cents an hour to work for me."

That sounded good to me because in 1926, thirty-five cents an hour was pretty good money. I worked for him all that year and made him a hand. I made him a good hand. But he never liked me and was always distant.

A man across the road from us had a little farm, and Old Man Greenlee didn't like him either. One day he and I started out in the truck, when he stopped and jumped on this fellow. And this kid told him,

"I'm not even twenty-one. I'm only eighteen years old. I don't want to fight you."

He didn't say any more, but was mad when he came back to me where I was sitting in the truck. He asked,

"Do you consider yourself a man?"

"I sure as hell do!"

"What would you do if somebody came up and cussed you out like I did him? What would you do?"

"The first damn thing he'd have to do is whip me, and then he could call me all the things you called him, cause I wouldn't stand for it. He might whip me, but he damn sure would have a fight. I'd fight you. So don't ever try it with me if you want to get along with me."

Well, he never did. But he did terrible things to his own kids and everybody else.

The year I worked for him, he had about twenty head of mules that he farmed with. The mules ate headed maize, which he kept in a barn crib as well as big ricks outside the barn. Along in May 1926, he got me to help him make a big batch of home brew. Now home brew needed a little sugar in it to give it some kick, but he wanted a big kick, so he put extra sugar into each bottle. We ended up with about fifty bottles, and I asked,

"Where are you going to hide all this stuff?"

"Aw," he said, "let's hide it in that crib of maize."

So we went in there and scratched back, putting two or three bottles here and two or three bottles there until they were scattered over the whole crib of maize. Well, maize heats up in hot weather, particularly if it is confined in a barn. Consequently, the bottles began to boil in that maize.

One day we had just come in from the field for lunch, had turned the teams loose, and had gone up to the house to eat. While eating, we heard something go baaaang! He looked over at me and I looked over at him and said,

"I don't know what that was."

Pretty soon another one went bang and then another, and another. Then it sounded like Cox's army going off. Of course, Mrs. Greenlee didn't go for any of that.

She jumped all over him about it. We went down to the maize crib and found three bottles that hadn't blown up. He had a well where the water was cold about twenty feet below the ground. He put a rope on a galvanized bucket with the beer in it and lowered it into the water to cool off the beer. We tied the rope and left it until noon the next day.

When we came in from the field the next day, he said,

"Boy! We're gonna have at least a glass of beer out of this!"

He drew up the bucket saying,

"I don't know, this stuff might be kinda wild. I'm gonna catch it in this bucket."

He started to open the first bottle and the cap blew off before he could get the bottle turned far enough, and it just went swoosh! right out over the top of the bucket. He got a very little in the bucket. Opening the next one very slowly, he held the neck down inside the bucket where the beer just foamed and foamed and foamed, finally emptying completely into the bucket. When he started to open the third bottle, the cap suddenly blew off, hit the bucket, and turned it upside down. He didn't get to drink a drop of beer. You talk about somebody mad! He would have blamed it on me if he could have. Oh, he was a booger to be around. One day I said to him,

"I don't understand anybody like you that's always mad at everybody. I never see you in a good mood with anybody or treating anybody decent. You're always mad."

He tried to excuse himself by saying,

"I'm always mad from the time I start a crop until I finish it."

"Yeah," I replied, "If you'll just look around you,

you will see what's the matter. Ever since I have known you, you have started a crop on the second day of February. You got a habit of doing that, and you gotta stick to it when you haven't even finished gathering last year's crop."

That year we made a little money out of our cotton crop. In December of that year, our son James was born. Then Rita and I got a chance to rent a place by ourselves. I bought four head of bald-faced horses and had enough farm equipment with what I could beg, borrow, or steal from the neighbors. As far as the work was concerned, I had plenty of capacity for that. In addition to farming, we raised a bunch of chickens, but I got disgusted having to live so close to her father who was always giving her a lot of trouble. She didn't like it, and I didn't like it either.

We decided to go to Magdalena, New Mexico. Lyo had sent us a letter saying that he and Dad were there. We had bought this old Model T Ford, and I finally put some curtains on it. It was late winter and very cold, especially around Capitan, New Mexico. We set a kerosene heater in the floor to try to keep warm. It kept us warm all right, but the fumes were so bad, we had to open the curtains.

When we got to Magdalena, Dad said,

"I know where you can go to work."

"Fine! I'm ready."

"I know a fellow that's got a service station, and he wants a hand."

I worked there for quite a while. But in the meantime, Dad always had his hand in the liquor business one way or another. I don't know where he got his whiskey, but he sold it to me at wholesale, and I sold it at retail to tourists who came to the service station. The boss gave me a lot of static about it, so I quit and got a job in a pool hall. I worked there quite a while, getting paid twenty dollars every day.

During this time, Dad bought a store in Quemado, New Mexico. He told me,

"If you want to come out here, I can get you on at the highway department."

Since it would pay a lot more money than I was making, I worked there until the following spring. About that time George Cox, an old cowboy I had known for some time, came by and said,

"Let's go to Bisbee."

"What for?"

"They're hiring men down in the mines."

"Oh, are they?"

"Yeah, let's go down there and see if we can go to work."

We headed for Bisbee in his old straight-eight Studebaker. His brother always remarked to me,

"If George had thirteen hands, he'd drive with one and hold on with the other twelve."

Anyway, we got to Bisbee, put in our applications and went to work immediately. We checked into a hotel where the food was not fit to eat, but dozens of people were trying to eat. We went to a restaurant down the street to see if they would let us eat an evening meal and fix us a lunch for the next day. We could get breakfast anywhere. At the restaurant, a man who looked like a Mexican waited on us and George told him what we wanted in Spanish. This guy looked kinda of blank and said,

"Wait a minute."

He called his boss up front who was a white guy. George spoke in English,

"What we want is to eat supper here every day and get somebody to fix us a lunch to take to work each morning. We got a place to stay."

The boss agreed, "Yeah, we can do that."

The Mexican, who couldn't speak a word of Spanish, spoke up,

"Why didn't you say that in the first place?"

We went to work in the mines and changed places to live a time or two. I had left Rita and James in Quemado. When I got my first paycheck a month later, I sent for them to come to Bisbee. I did really well working in the mines. I worked bonus. I just worked my head off. I made good money and was working with my Uncle Jim. He was a good partner and a good worker, and he'd put in a good word for me. I went right on up from mucker to miner right away. They paid better wages than elsewhere. I worked there all that year until about July the next year when people were being laid off right and left. The stock market had crashed in September 1929, and this was 1930. The company was laying off men who had worked there for fifteen years, and I had only been there a year and a half. I kept thinking every day would be my last. I had a lot of stress just wondering from day-to-day if I would have a job. To complicate matters, Lyo had a habit of moving in with us when he was out of a job, and he had been staying with us for a month doing nothing while I worked the night shift. Rita and I weren't getting along very well anyway. We had a lot of difficulties that really didn't amount to a whole lot, but we were both kids, and neither one of us had many adult ideas about anything. When things didn't go right, they just didn't go right.

One day I went into the change room and was going to change clothes to go to work down in the mine. The change room was hot and smelled bad. So did my work clothes, which felt like fire when I put them on. I just walked around to the foreman and stated,

"I want a two-weeks furlough."

The astonished man repeated,

"Two-weeks furlough! You mean you're going to ask for a two-weeks furlough when people everywhere are being laid off?"

"Yeah."

"Well, don't blame me if you don't have a job when you get back."

"I won't."

He wrote me a slip for a two-week furlough, and I took it to the employment office. I knew the employment agent, who had an unusually good memory. He knew Dad when he worked there, what day he started to work, what day he left, and he knew my two brothers who had worked there in the past. He asked about them and what they were doing. After I told him where they were, he assured me,

"Well, Lee, come back in two weeks, and your job will be waiting for you."

I never did go back. I just kept going. Rita and I were having a lot of trouble, and I took her back to Old Man Greenlee's place. She was mad at me, and I couldn't talk to her, and that made me mad. I knew she had a lot of her dad's blood. He was overbearing, and she was overbearing. So I said,

"To heck with it!"

I turned around and walked out the door and never did go back. I got into the car with Lyo and headed down the road to Tahoka. Sixteen dollars was all the money I had because I had given the rest to Rita. I didn't know where I was going or what I was going to do, and Lyo didn't have any ideas either. When we got to town, he saw a jacket in a store window that cost sixteen dollars, and he wanted it. I cautioned,

"Lyo, the generator is out on the car, and I've got to get a new generator. Where do you think you're going to get the money for that jacket?"

"I don't give a damn where you get the money. I want you to give me that sixteen dollars so I can buy that jacket."

"I'm not going to give it to you!"

We almost had a fight right there and would have if we hadn't been in the street. When we got to the car, he wanted to drive, so I let him drive. Then he drove just as fast and reckless as he could 'til I finally reached down and took the key out of the ignition. Then I snapped,

"Let's get out right here and get it on, 'cause I'm not gonna put up with this nonsense. I'm not gonna be killed by someone acting like an idiot."

He didn't want to fight and moved over to the passenger side, and I drove us to Quemada where Dad and Reuben were.

The three of us, Lyo, Reuben, and I did some things together, some of which we weren't supposed to. Dad was having a tough time trying to run a service station and garage during the day and a dance hall on Saturday nights. He was far into debt and didn't have any money. He wanted some beef, and we didn't have any money to buy beef. So Lyo, Reuben, and I went back over the mountains and found some guy's cattle and butchered one of his calves. We put the beef into the back of our old car and took it home. We had beef.

Tom Lee, father of Dud Lee

CHAPTER 4
PROHIBITION

Since Dad's other businesses were not doing very well, he began to distill whiskey during Prohibition in August of 1930. Being out of work, Reuben and I joined him in this illegal business. The severe unemployment of the Great Depression changed the way people thought about a lot things. For millions of folks, just having enough to eat and somewhere to call home were small luxuries. People desperate to survive will do things they ordinarily would not do. And a lot of decent people violated the Prohibition Act even though it carried a maximum fine of $10,000 and five years in prison. Although I was only twenty-two years old, I felt I could handle anything that came along.

Reuben and I helped my dad by knocking heads out of barrels and kegs and whatever else he needed us to do. He colored his whiskey by burning the insides of the barrels. After he charred the insides of the barrels, we would put the heads back in and fill them with whiskey. He never used any kind of additives. The whiskey was just a natural charcoal color.

Dad had a small lake nearby that was just big enough to accomplish what he wanted to do with the whiskey. He would leave a little air space in the kegs and barrels and roll them out into the lake. As the wind was blowing the kegs to the opposite side of the lake, the waves would rock them. The more the kegs were rocked, the more the whiskey was aged. In this manner he made the best whiskey anybody ever drank.

Dad had a fifty-gallon barrel of whiskey that he had to get out of sight. So he told Reuben and me to go dig a hole on the upper side of the lake where it was sandy and full of weeds. We dug a hole that we thought was deep enough to bury two mules, but when we rolled the barrel into the hole, about of foot of it was sticking up on the air. So then the chore was to get the barrel back out. We got poles to pry under it and dug a little dirt out on one side so it wouldn't be such a steep pull. It was such a job that we made sure that it was deep enough next time by measuring the barrel and measuring the hole.

Afterwards, there wasn't much else to do, so Reuben and I decided to sell some whiskey. Dad would sell it to us for ten dollars a gallon and we would double the price. We could get twenty bottles out of a gallon and sell them for two dollars each.

We decided to sell five gallons of our whiskey in Mountainair, New Mexico. We still had about two bottles left when we were somewhere around Socorra. As we were driving along, this old Model-T Ford with its top off came sailing around us. It was occupied by a couple of cowboys. The one on the passenger side had his foot propped up on the windshield and was leaning back smoking a cigarette.

Ruben suggested, "Let's stop those cowboys and give them a drink of good whiskey."

I replied, "That sounds like a good idea."

So we went around them and waved them to stop. When they came alongside of us, we asked,

"Would you fellows like a drink of good whiskey?"
"Why, shore!" they exclaimed.

So I handed the passenger a bottle. He had on boots and spurs. You would have thought that he had just stepped out of a corral somewhere. He took the bottle and tasted it first. He was wearing wide suspenders. Then he turned his suspender around to reveal a badge emblazoned "Sheriff." I thought, "Uh oh!" Then I took a good look at it again, and it proclaimed "State of Texas."

I laughed at him saying, "Well, you're in the wrong jurisdiction, aren't you?"

He laughed and admitted, "Yeah, I guess I am. I just wanted to see how you would take it." Then he inquired, "Where in the world do you get that kind of whiskey? I never tasted any kind of whiskey like that."

I confided, "We got plenty of it. If you want it, we'll get you some."

He responded, "Well, I'll tell you what you do. I'll buy twenty gallons if you'll take it to Pampa, Texas."

I agreed. Then he told me how to deliver it.

"Y'all go down to the end of a dead-end street. At the last house on the street, there will be a garage. There is some junk in the garage, but the doors are open. Put that whiskey in the corner and go to the bank and introduce yourselves to the president. Y'all tell the banker who you are and mention my name and he will pay you."

"Fine!" I concluded, "We'll do that."

So a day or two later, we loaded our whiskey into a little borrowed roadster with a rumble seat. First, we put the whiskey into our bedrolls. Next, we rolled up blankets and quilts and put them at each end. Then we tied the whole thing together and laid it in the rumble seat. We put our bridles and spurs underneath and fastened my saddle on top and make it look like two western cowboys traveling.

In those days, people were checked at every state line to see what they were taking into the next state. When we got stopped at the state line, we got out while the inspectors checked us out. They saw that our car was from New Mexico and asked,

"Where are you going?"

"We're going to Amarillo," we lied. "Just going to look for a job in an outfit around Canyon."

"Fine, now what have you got in here?" The inspector demanded.

"I lied again, "Nothing. Just a bedroll."

"What's under it," he insisted.

I hedged saying, "I don't know, not much of anything."

J.W. (Dud) Lee, taken in 1933, Paradise, Arizona.

It was pretty heavy because there were twenty gallons of booze in there. But Ruben got on one end and I got on the other and we heaved that bedroll out of there so as to make it look as though it was light. The inspector ordered us to set it out on the ground. But then he looked inside, and seeing nothing of any consequence conceded,

"Naw, you're

all right. Go ahead."

We went on to Pampa, and sure enough, on arriving, we found the street, went down it, and everything was just like the sheriff said. We set the keg in the corner of the garage and then went to the bank and asked for the president. We were led back into his office. We told him what our names were and that a guy who was a sheriff had sent us. We told him we were supposed to collect some money from him.

"Oh yeah! Yeah!" He acknowledged, "I know who you are. How much did you bring?"

"Twenty gallons," I replied.

He just said, "O.K." and counted out four hundred dollars and handed it to us. We then left for Quemada and paid Dad for his half.

We decided that worked pretty good, and that we would sell some more. Quemado is a long way from Paradise, Arizona, but that is where we really wanted to go. So we got two twenty-gallon kegs from Dad and took off for Paradise. Meanwhile, Lyo had returned to Quemado and we took him with us.

When we got to Lordsburg, a heavy rain had caused some street flooding. One of the deep dips in the street was running full of swift water and had everybody backed up on each side. Since we had forty gallons of whiskey in the back of our old car, Lyo was scared.

"What if somebody gets into that car?" He asked.

I responded, "I've got the key, and they ain't going to tear it up to get in there. Nobody is even going to look in there because they don't have a search warrant."

Looking at the running water, one old boy in a little light car said, "Well, I think I can make it across if I hit it fast enough."

So he backed off and made a fast run at it. When he hit that water, it stopped him like a brick wall. Then he just sunk down with the water almost over the top of the car. He crawled through a window just before the car washed off the road and out of sight.

Some guy on the other side with a big truck told the man, "If you'll get out in the water and tie on the bumper with this chain, I'll pull you out of that water."

In this way, they got the car pulled out and let the water drain. Of course, it couldn't be driven until it was taken to a garage and cleaned up.

All this time we just sat there watching the water while Lyo was having a nervous fit.

"What are we going to do?" Let's turn around and go the other way."

I said, "We're not going anywhere until this water runs down. Then we are going on to Paradise. We're not going to create any suspicion whatever."

Finally, the water had run down so that I could wade across it with the water a little above my knees. This old guy with the truck said,

"I'll tell you what. If you want to try to make it, get in the car and I will hook on to you before you even start."

I replied, "Fine! That sounds good to me."

So we took the chain across to the other side and tied it to my bumper. He gunned the engine of his truck and pulled us right through the water while I kept my engine running fast to keep the water out of the tail pipe. We helped him get three more cars across before we left.

Nearing Paradise, we cached our whiskey in some brush in a canyon up in the Chiricahua Mountains. Then we went on to Paradise and joined up with my brother Bud. We would fill up ten or fifteen of our little brown bottles and take them to dances every Saturday night and sell four or five gallons during a dance. Of course, the people didn't drink it all right then, but they would take it home with them. This is how we made our living right then. We stayed in Paradise, but would go to Rodeo, New Mexico, about twenty miles away to dances or something where we could sell our whiskey. But we

Paradise, Arizona.

were running out of whiskey and were going to have to do something else.

That's when Bud, Reuben, and I split up. Reuben was just a twenty-three-year-old kid, but you would have thought he was an old alcoholic. He would wake up every morning with a headache and had to have a drink. Well, heck, he was drinking up all the whiskey we had left for his headaches. He would have headaches during the day, too. I never drank the stuff myself. Bud finally got a job stacking hay for an old rancher named Mr. Hons.

Two or three days later he came back and was kind of throwing out his chest and bragging,

"I'm the only one working around here and making

a living, and you guys are laying around on your butts and not doing anything, and I don't care much for that. You guys are going to have to get you a job or something."

He had forgotten that I had furnished the money for everything up until then, and I furnished the car. He didn't have one.

I snapped, "Well, if that's the way you feel about it, I'll just take my nickel out!"

I left and didn't see or talk to Bud again for nearly fifty years. I gave up bootlegging for good. That's when I ran into my cousin Dale and learned to hunt mountain lions.

Dud Lee, Reuben Wright, and Tom Lee
Pie Town, New Mexico, 1937

CHAPTER 5
BEGINNER'S LUCK

When my cousin Dale, who lived across the creek from me, found out I was leaving, he came over and asked,

"How'd you like to help me exercise some dogs and get them ready to hunt mountain lions?"

I replied, "I guess I may as well. I haven't got anything else to do."

The first few times we took the dogs out of the pen, you would have thought they were going to run forty miles before they looked back. But after running a mile, they were all sore footed and couldn't walk, and we had to coax them back home. By that time, they were ready to just lie down. Of course, each day we would take them a little farther and a little farther until they could go all day and all night. There wasn't any end to it after they got toughened up.

Dale had wanted just the two of us to hunt lions, but changed his plans. Ernest was the oldest one in the Lee family, and he did all the corresponding to dudes who wanted to hunt lions for sport, using us as guides. Also, in those days, the government had a bounty on mountain lions since they were a serious menace to live stock on ranches in the area. We had to average two lions a month to work for the government. That wasn't too difficult back in those days in that part of the country.

So on the first of September 1930, I started hunting lions with my cousin Vincent, while Dale and Clell went to New Mexico.

We rode and we rode. And we hunted and we rode all through the Chiricahua Mountains, but it was October 15 before we hit a trail that we could run. Finally, as we were going around a mountain, we saw this lion track in the snow that seemed to be as big as a hat because it was all melted out. I followed it a ways on foot in places where there was no snow. Then the dogs lost the trail. We were going along the tops of some bluffs about twenty feet high. The dogs went along there but made a loop and couldn't go any farther. They circled back and that was the end of the trail.

While looking around, I noticed a tall pine tree down at the bottom of those bluffs. Looking over the edge, I could see tracks at the bottom of this tree, which was down in the snow. That lion had jumped off the bluff onto the top of the tree and then had gone down the tree. That bluff was pretty hard to conquer, but the dogs kind of got wise. They went way up until they found a place to make it down to the bottom. I followed the dogs, but they got down before I did and went back to the tree to pick up the trail, which took them down the mountain a ways. Near the bottom of the canyon, they came upon a deer killed by the lion. The lion had just been there that morning. The dogs didn't stop there. They hit a hot trail across the bottom and up the other side of the mountain on the North Slope. Here, the snow was knee deep, making it difficult for me to walk through it because I was climbing up bluffs and rocks. Coming up against a ledge, I threw my rifle up on top and climbed up after it. When I finally got upon the top, I could see the dogs barking at the lion sitting up in an old gnarled tree. I went behind a nearby thicket and opened up my rifle because it was full of snow. After cleaning out the snow, I threw a shell into the chamber and walked around to where the lion was. He was watching me and watching the dogs, and watching me and watching the dogs. I picked a spot where I had a pretty good open shot at him and fired. At the time, I didn't know where I had hit him, but it was a deadly shot. The bullet went in under his eye and came out the back of his head. The lion fell out of the tree and just disappeared over the cliff. I didn't know where he went because the ground was all covered in snow. I moved closer to get a better look and found myself staring straight down about three hundred feet. Naturally, the dogs wanted to go down where the lion went, and I was having a hard time keeping them back from the edge of the cliff. At first, I couldn't see the lion, but growing out the side of the bluff was one of these old manzanita trees, or bushes, which are just like iron. You can stand on a twig the size of your finger without breaking it. The lion was draped over this manzanita tree just like he might have been draped over a clothesline. I thought he was about one hundred and fifty feet down and about one hundred and fifty feet up from the bottom and didn't know what I was going to do. While I was just staring and wondering what to do, the lion started sliding. Pretty soon he slid all the way to the bottom.

I started climbing back up the mountain where Vince was waiting and watching what had been going on. He was at the top of Cave Creek Falls, which is about two hundred feet high and drops straight down onto huge rocks that slope off into a canyon. In my excitement of having shot my first lion, I was hollering and talking to Vince.

He hollered back, "You go on down and get the lion.

I'm going to go around and hit the South Fork Canyon below. I'll come up South Fork as far as I can with the horses, and you can start coming down with the lion and the dogs. I'll meet you."

The first mountain lion Dud ever killed.
From l. to r.: Dud Lee and Clell Lee.

I yelled, "O.K." and started picking my way through loose rocks and brush to get down to where the lion was. Below there, Cave Creek runs off into a canyon. Here, the falls are sloped instead of straight down. One of the rocks in the falls was about thirty feet from top to bottom and lay at a sixty-degree incline. Once I got down there, getting back up was out of the question. I knew the dogs wouldn't follow me down. So first, I threw the lion down. Two of the dogs ran up and hit the slick rock and slid on down. I pushed off the other three dogs and then slid myself off into the icy water.

Believe you me that water was cold! I slid down two or three more rocks like the first one before coming to one about thirty feet high that was straight down. Of course, I couldn't take that. So I had to rim around up a hillside above these falls. The going was hard because of loose rocks. Besides, I was completely water soaked and very cold. Everything I stepped on would slide, and I sure didn't want to fall down into the canyon, which was pretty rough. I finally reached Vince and the horses just before dark. We built a big fire to dry out my clothes. Then we loaded the lion on a horse and went home. That was the biggest lion that the Lee brothers ever killed. He measured six feet, one inch, and weighed one hundred fifty-six pounds. He was a monster, a big lion. Of course, we had some pictures made the next morning because I was really thrilled about my first lion hunt and killing my first lion.

CHAPTER 6
WAMPUS KITTY

My cousin Vince had a little problem. He drank quite a bit, but he was one of the best hunters I ever hunted with. Because he was so good, he really taught me how to hunt. We hunted together and killed two or three lions along the way. Then we went over to the south end of the Chiricahua Mountains to Kendall Ranch to use it as a base for hunting lions in that area. We camped out back up in the hills. Although we had our own horses, we didn't have enough to ride them every day; so the ranch furnished us with some of their horses. They helped us out all they could.

After we had been camped out for about two weeks, Vince decided to go into Rodeo to get some groceries. Well, I never saw Vince for about a week. He just got on one of those binges. After he left, I continued to hunt lions alone.

One day I jumped this lion, and the dogs treed it without running it very far. It was an old female. I killed that lion, and then we jumped one that had three kittens. The dogs put one of the kittens up a tree, and I killed it too. Then I took all my kills down to the ranch and called my cousin Ernest to come pick them up. I didn't even bother to skin them. Ernest could skin them after he took them home. I wanted to keep hunting.

Ernest asked, "Were there some more kittens up

there?"

"I'm sure there were," I replied.

Then he suggested, "I'll bring some traps. There's a kill up there. Go up there and check that kill and see if the lions are still coming back to it. Those kittens will come back to that kill, and you can set some traps up there and maybe catch 'em."

So he brought the traps, and I took them up into the mountain. Sure enough, the kittens had been coming back to the kill, but they had just about eaten all of it. But I knew where there was another kill that a male lion had made. He had eaten off it but never returned. So I cut the hindquarter off it and tied it to a limb at the same place where the other kill was and where the kittens kept coming back and eating on it. In this way, I kept on feeding them this other kill.

Well, one morning, I had a kitten in a trap. The horse I was riding belonged to the ranch and had never been around any lions. He didn't know anything about lions and didn't like the smell of them. I took this kitten, which weighed about forty pounds, and tied his mouth shut and tied all four feet together. This way, I could hook him on my arm. I had him hooked on my arm when I went back to get on my horse. When that horse smelled that lion, he just tore up the world trying to get away. He was running and jerking so hard that I had to throw down the kitten. I finally got him stopped and under control some distance from the lion and tied him to some trees. Then I went back to get my kitten.

There was an old pine tree nearby that had a dead snag sticking out about as high as I could reach. I just hung the kitten over this limb up in the tree and returned to get my horse.

Now, from the top of the mountain, there was a trail. I was right on top of the ridge. Going from there down to the ranch, this trail zigzagged back and forth across that little canyon so that riding up or down wouldn't be so steep. That canyon was pretty steep for anyone going straight down. My intent was to go back down this trail. I rode back up to get the kitten in the tree. The horse could smell the lion, but he was looking for him on the ground. He was just looking and stomping and jumping around. Finally, we got close enough to the tree that I could reach out and hook that kitten on my arm and pull him over to me. Whenever I did, that old horse left! Of course, I went with him! He straightened out that trail. He went straight down that canyon. He ran just as hard as he could, and I couldn't hold him or handle him in any way. I was just hanging on to the horse, hanging on to the lion, and fighting brush and trees that we ripped through.

After we had dashed about a half-mile down the canyon, the horse calmed down. I guess he thought he wasn't going to get caught by this lion. Upon taking the lion to the ranch, I went back up the mountain and caught another kitten, but it would be two more days before Vince showed up.

After that wild ride, I could catch a lion, throw it down, and lead that old horse up to it and throw the lion in the saddle. I could get on the horse with the lion, and the horse would never untrack. He became a good horse for hunting lions.

He proved it about a month later when I hit a lion trail going up another canyon that was pretty close to the first one. I trailed while the dogs went straight up the mountain. I went as far as I could on horseback, and then started walking. There are many places in the Chiricahuas that are too rugged for horses. You have to go on foot. Tying my horse to a tree, I started climbing. Soon, the dogs were out of hearing.

I was puffing and snorting and hurrying and climbing that mountain and slipping and sliding with it. After climbing about a half a mile, I stopped and listened because I thought I heard a dog. I went a little farther, and again I thought I heard a dog. The more I walked, the plainer I could hear the dogs. They had run on to this lion feeding on a kill. In his attempt to get away from the dogs, the lion came right back over the hill where he had gone up. He came within about fifty feet of me and continued on down toward my horse. Although the lion went right by him, the horse did not try to break loose.

The dogs were right behind the lion as he went down the bottom of the canyon and then started up the other side where the dogs treed him. Not wanting to climb that side of the mountain on foot, I was anxious to shoot the lion before he could jump out and run again. When I got to the lion, he was in a tree about fifty feet from the ground. He saw me, and I saw him sticking his head under the limb, looking for a place to jump. The dogs were barking around the base of the tree, and the lion was just looking for a place where he could get through the dogs.

I decided to shoot at the lion's head. That way, if I missed him, I would hit the limb and lion wouldn't jump out wounded in front of all the dogs. A wounded lion will tear up a bunch of dogs. Whenever a lion is shot out of a tree, the dogs will cover the pile right there when he hits the ground. Well, I shot at him, and he kind of wilted a little bit, but he just sat there with his head hanging down, still in the same place. So I drew another bead and shot him again. That time he fell out of the tree. Of course, he was dead when he hit the ground. I put him on my horse and checked him over. I had shot him right in the throat, and both bullets went into the same hole and came out about an inch apart in the back of his head. So he was dead twice! Putting him on my horse, I took him to the ranch for Ernest to turn over to the government in exchange for another badly needed one-hundred-and-twenty-five bucks.

Chapter 7
The Three C's

I quit lion hunting for awhile to work for the Civilian Conservation Corps (CCC) when the program first started in 1931. The idea behind this program was to put men to work during the depression. We were hired to do public works projects such as soil erosion control. We also built some beautiful nature trails in the Chiricahua Mountains, which are still there. I drove a truck to haul men to the various jobs. I never was the kind of guy to sit around and watch others work. Once when we went to a creek bed to gather rocks to haul, I got out of my truck and was loading rocks like everybody else when my boss came around and said,

"We've got twenty guys here to pick up rocks, and we've just one truck driver. So you just stay on the truck."

So driving the truck was not hard work, but it was boring because they had governors on the truck to keep it from going very fast. One day while I was hauling a load of fence posts off a mountain there in the Chiricahuas, the road was pretty steep and a little crooked. I let the old truck get to rolling pretty good and jammed it into second gear, and that apparatus that they had on there to control the speed was shot. After that I could drive about as fast as I wanted to.

But I really didn't care for truck driving all that much.

I wanted to get back into the saddle. So they put me to doing trail work in the mountains. In addition to my horse, I had five pack mules to carry supplies to men working on the trails that were built on a seven-degree incline which made it easy for people to get around.

One day I was putting new shoes on these mules and some were not gentle. They were gentle enough for packing, but they didn't like to have their feet picked up. I had a kid holding a mule while I was trying to put a shoe on him. Shoot, he couldn't hold the mule steady enough for me to put the shoe on him. So I said,

"Here, you put the shoe on him and let me hold him."

Well, I got hold of both ears of this mule and jammed one of them in my mouth and shut down on it with my teeth. I pulled him down and was holding him pretty good when all of a sudden he slung his head and jumped, and zip, he slipped away from me. I noticed that I had a mouth full of hair and started to spit it out. But I had bitten off about three inches of that danged mule's ear. They almost fired me over that. They didn't like having that mule mutilated, but we got him shod.

I went on up to where the workmen were camped out and arrived well before lunch. The cook was a good kid named Beans, who was always full of fun and pretty witty. He said,

"Since they all won't be here for another hour, let's eat lunch, and you can get started back down the mountains."

That suited me. He got out something like mulligan stew, and then he opened a can of peaches, which we ate. About that time the trail troop came on down. When they had finished eating, one of them walked over to the edge of the hill, saw the discarded peach can, and said,

"Hey, did we have peaches for lunch?"

Beans said, "Naw, you didn't. I did."

Beans had his own way of controlling things. We had one guy who was a good boxer and had boxed in the ring around the country. One evening in the bunkhouse, Beans, as usual, was kidding around and giving everybody trouble. This boxer said,

"If you don't shut up, I'm going to beat the tar out of you."

Beans just calmly replied, "You'd be going around behind the barracks saying, 'Who'd a thought it, too.'"

Of course, everybody roared because Beans couldn't whip his shirt if you threw it on the gate.

Clell Lee and Dud Lee
Paradise, Arizona, 1931

CHAPTER 8
ARIZONA LIONS IN CALIFORNIA

In the spring of 1932, I quit the three C's and went back to hunting lions. We were getting pretty short because that $125 per month from the government not only took care of me, but also Ernest, his wife, Clell, Dell, and his mother. It was hard for six people to live on that. Clell and I decided to go to California because the state would pay $75 and Orange County would pay another $25 for every lion that was killed. Clell and I decided to guarantee ourselves $200.

So we went out into the Chiricahuas and killed two lions. We had an old Dodge car that had a lid that opened to a compartment behind the back of the seat. It was about ten inches wide and two feet deep. Anyone who didn't know it was there would never notice it. After we killed these two lions, we packed them in dry ice and put them into this compartment. We had made a box on the back of the car and screened it to haul our dogs. Up above the dogs, we had a compartment that had canned goods and other stuff to eat. We figured we could haul two small horses in a trailer behind the car. So we borrowed a trailer from Ernest and started out. Unfortunately, the horses weren't very sensible because they kicked out the sides of the trailer after about six miles. So we just parked the trailer, took the horses back to Paradise, and left again for California.

Of course, Clell and I got stopped for inspection at the California State line. Because of the dogs, the inspectors just kind of looked around inside the car with this old truck bed on it and waved us on across.

By now, it was summertime, and we made camp on top of a mountain, not far from a creek with running water. Clell had turned the dogs loose and was fixing something to eat while I went to the creek for a couple of buckets of water. Coming back, I don't know what happened, but those crazy dogs saw me coming and headed my way. They would eat you alive if they didn't know you, and they hadn't recognized me at all. At first, I thought they were just playing, but I waited until I saw they were serious. I set my buckets down and said,

"What in the hell are you doing!"

Recognizing my voice, they dropped their tails and went behind me back to camp. We stayed there that night and the next day. The next night we loaded one of those lions onto the bumper and drove it down by a dude ranch at the bottom of the mountain and told them we had killed a lion up there. But before we ever went up into the mountain, we had stopped by the ranch and let them know that the great lion hunters had arrived.

We told the people at the ranch that we had to have witnesses that we killed the lion up in the mountain. One kid spoke up,

"Heck yeah, I'll tell them I saw you shoot it if they ask me."

But we weren't questioned about witnesses. We brought in one lion one day and the other one the next day. We thought we could just collect our money and head back to Paradise. It didn't turn out that way. The authorities accepted the lions all right, but a guy at the courthouse stunned us.

"You'll have to wait thirty days for your money."

We didn't know what we were going to do since we had no money. And since we didn't expect to be in California long, we had very little food—just a couple of cans of spinach, some bread, and canned milk. For a day or two, we ate bread sprinkled with sugar and soaked in canned milk. Clell was pretty well down in the dumps and irritated about the whole situation. I tried to cheer him up.

"I don't know what we are going to do, but we will do something. Don't worry about it. In thirty or forty years, you'll look back and think this is funny."

However, when I told this story at a Lee reunion in 1978, Clell still wasn't laughing.

One morning we thought maybe we could kill another lion. Going up into a canyon, we saw a sign reading, "Private Property, No Trespassing." Heck, we were in the mountains. It wasn't anybody's private property. I knew the government owned the land. We kept on going. Finally, we got to a little mining concern where two men had a little trestle hauling dirt out and dumping it over the hill. One was a tall old man, the other a big young Jew. When they saw us, the big guy started in,

"Can't you guys read? That says 'Private Property' down there."

"Well," I said, "I don't think so. I think it belongs to the government."

"We got this country leased. We own it, and we don't want no trespassers."

"I'll tell you what. We're hunting for the government, and we are going to hunt up here whether you like it or don't like it."

"Well, you ain't gonna hunt up here, I'll tell you that. And if you are hunting lions, how do I know you might shoot at a lion and hit me?"

Clell took up the argument,

"If we do, you're going to have to be up in a tree with the lion, and I don't think you are going to be up there."

We argued about five minutes. Clell and I were carrying our rifles. Clell was already unhappy about our predicament, so losing his patience, he set his rifle against a bank and said,

"Dud, let's whip these sons-of-bitches and get on our way."

"O.K.," I said, "You get the old man, and I will take this big Jew."

I knew the old man wouldn't last long, and then we would both take on the big guy.

"Naw," he said, "We're not going to do that. You get the old man, and I will get the big Jew."

I protested, "I'm not going to be whipped by that old man."

Clell replied, "You just hold him off 'til I get through with this one."

Then the old man spoke up,

"Now wait a minute, fellows. Wait a minute. We ought to be able to talk this out some way."

Clell snorted, "Yeah, I thought we could too, to start with, but you fellows didn't seem to want to talk."

They finally agreed that it was all right for us to hunt in that area. After we all calmed down, we got to talking to them and they turned out to be pretty good fellows. They would come by our camp and ask if we wanted anything from town. Of course, we did, but we didn't have any money, so we always said we didn't need anything.

This dude ranch was about a mile away, and I used to walk over there in the evening. There was a place outside with a big fireplace with three openings and a smokestack. Benches ringed three sides where people could sit and tell lies. Ever once in a while somebody would sing a few songs. In those days, I was a very good singer. In fact, all the Lees, as well as the Wrights on my mother's side, were good musicians. By the time I was sixteen, I had been to a few singing schools.

One time, I went with my dad, my stepmother, and my Uncle Elmer to Brownwood, Texas, to a singing convention. That was the biggest congregation I had ever seen. There must have been four or five thousand people in this huge auditorium. A piano rested on a rostrum down front with tiers rising behind it where the choir was seated. There must have been a hundred and fifty people in each section of the choir. When my uncle went to join the choir, I just got a songbook and went with him into the tenor section. We sang all morning. After a noon break, we started up again. James D. Vaughn, from Nashville, ramrodded the meeting. He had published the songbooks and written some of the songs. About two o'clock, I was having a good time just singing my heart out. I noticed that James Vaughn would walk up and down the aisles in the choir and occasionally stop and just listen. Once he stopped right where I was and listened. Later, he announced that he was going to pick a quartet out of the choir and see what kind of music he could get. He picked a man with a powerful bass voice, a woman to sing alto, another man to sing lead, and me to sing tenor. We got a standing ovation. That was the biggest thing that had ever happened to me in my life. Later, James Vaughn asked me to go to Nashville with him. He said,

"I'll make a singer out of you and also make you a lot of money, because you've got a beautiful voice and you handle it well."

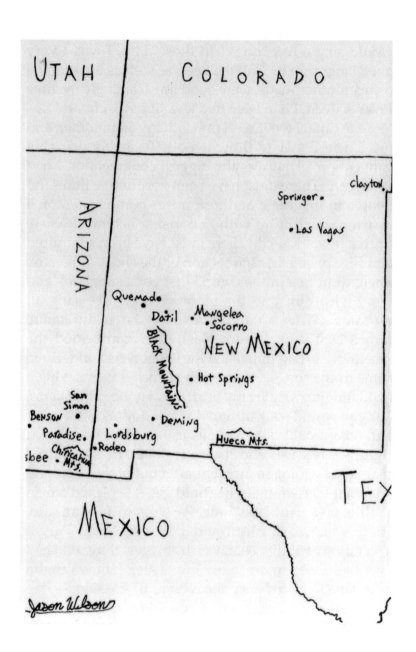

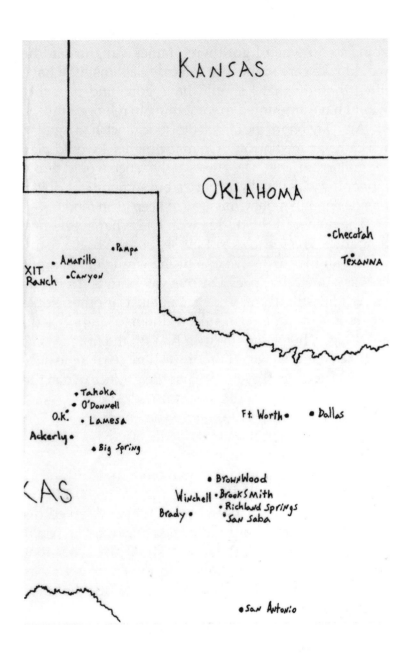

I didn't go because, well, I was only sixteen and had never been away from home and didn't know how to take care of myself. Besides, I didn't know what I was going to do when I got there. James Vaughn said he would take care of me, but I decided against it. I have often thought that I should have gone and probably would have amounted to something in religious music.

Anyway, one of the kids at the dude ranch had a guitar, which he let me borrow. On many nights, I would play the guitar and sing. The guests at the ranch would throw money my way, usually a quarter, but sometimes a dollar. I made enough money this way to keep us in food.

The owner of the dude ranch had what everybody thought was a terribly bad horse, but the horse really wasn't all that bad. But one of the wranglers thought he was something special by the way he rode the horse. He would snub him right up against another horse where he couldn't get his head down, or jump, or do anything. Then he would run him up the trail a ways and then come back and unsaddle him. That's the only way that horse had ever been handled. Once, when the wrangler returned from a ride, I asked,

"Can I borrow a saddle from somebody?"

A guy with a pretty good saddle offered,

"You can borrow mine."

"Thanks. I'm gonna ride that old horse."

I caught him out in the corral and put the saddle on him. I had a good hackamore on him and jerked his head around a few times and turned him out. He would buck in little jumps, but that was about all. I rode that horse up the trail and back and everybody was as surprised as the devil that anybody could ride the horse that was supposed to be a man killer.

This little incident made our visits to the dude ranch even more welcome.

CHAPTER 9
ROPING AND CAGING

The next winter, Dale and Clell hunted lions in Oregon but returned the following summer. Hunting lions in the summertime is not very practical. In the first place, it is too hot. Then, too, the dogs can't follow a dirt trail long enough because the dirt gets into their noses. Once in a while we might go out if we had a hot trail or had seen the lion. But most of the time in the summer, we just let the dogs rest.

So I punched cows for first one little rancher or another. Some had two- to four-hundred head of cattle. I worked quite a lot for my cousin Bill Lee. He had a little ranch with a couple hundred head of cattle. Bill knew a lot of ranchers around the country, and if they needed a hand, he would send me over. I usually punched cattle every summer, but lion hunting made more money.

The next winter, Dale and I put a new twist into our lion hunting. Ernest was still lining up hunting parties for dudes. He suggested that Dale and I catch lions and tie them up instead of shooting them. Whenever we had a hunting party of dudes, we always guaranteed them a lion. If they didn't get one, they didn't have to pay us anything. But we couldn't afford to take them on a hunt for nothing.

We had an old house in which we closed up the doors

and windows with heavy woven steel. When we caught a lion, we would tie him up and put him in that house. Then, if our hunting party hadn't got a lion toward the end of their trip, we got one out of the lion house. During the night we would put it into a cage and take it close to where we would be the next morning and release him. He wouldn't get far. The next morning we would pick up the lion's trail and let the dudes kill their lion. In this way, we pretty well had the lion hunting business sewed up. We tied up quite a number of lions and got into a lot of scrapes in doing so.

Once when Dale and I hunted, the dogs were pretty tired, and our horses were pretty well worked down. We didn't have too many horses. Since we were riding them about every second or third day in those mountains, they would get leg weary, making it difficult to get very much done. But Dale had a horse about thirty miles on the west side of the Chiricahua Mountains. He had left him there the year before to just run loose in the pasture.

He called the owner of the place and asked, "Is my horse Brutus still there?"

The man answered, "Yeah, he's still just running loose out in the pasture."

Then Dale added, "Well, we're a little short on horses right now, and I need to come and get him."

The man agreed saying, "He's your horse. Come on over. But he may be a little frisky because he hasn't been ridden in a long time."

"O.K.," Dale continued, "We'll leave right away."

So Dale and I mounted a couple of horses and headed over the mountains with four or five dogs. Well, on the way over, we hit a lion trail that was so hot that the dogs just ran off and left us. We finally caught up with them on the south side of a hill where there wasn't much snow—just a little patch now and then. And any lion track was just a big old splotch all melted out so that it was difficult to tell which direction he was going. After tracking for about two hours, we came out on the other side of the hill. Here, the tracks were plain enough in the snow to show that we were going the wrong way. So we called off the dogs and went back to the other end of the trail and followed it a ways. But the dogs were having trouble. By this time, it was getting late in the day, and we decided we had better go get the horse.

After picking up our horse, we wasted no time in heading back. During the night, we came upon a little house where an old man and old lady lived. We were tired and hungry, not having had anything to eat all day.

We asked the man, "Would you mind letting a couple of tired cowboys stay the rest of the night?"

He drawled, "Yeah, that's fine. Go ahead. We don't have much to eat around here. The wife cooked up enough for us, and I don't think there's much left, but you're welcome to what there is."

He was right. There wasn't much left, but Dale and I ate what there was. It didn't amount to much—just enough to whet our appetites. The horses had some hay, but the dogs didn't get anything to eat. They just lay around outside and waited until daylight.

The next morning, we went back to the lion's trail, which the dogs picked up immediately, and we trailed that sucker all day through some bluffs and up and down mountains. About an hour before sundown, we jumped him out of some bluffs. He ran down from the bluff and up a tree. Dale and I had a system where we took turns getting a lion out of a tree. He would climb a tree one time and I would climb a tree the next time to get the lion out. It was my turn to climb, so I went up the tree with my rope. I didn't get too close, and he didn't bother me too much. He just sat and snarled and spit. I put a loop on a long stick so I could reach over from my side of the tree to his side and try to get it around his neck. The sucker wouldn't be roped. He just ran down the tree and jumped out right in front of Dale and all the dogs. The dogs caught him about a hundred yards down the hill where they had a little battle. Of course, the dogs weren't going to fight him too much because they knew he hadn't been shot and was still alive and in good shape. While the dogs were worrying the lion, I came down the tree as fast as I could and helped Dale tie up the dogs because the lion was lying there on the ground—just kind of spitting and growling at the dogs.

Dale got his rifle and said, "I guess if that son-of-a-gun runs, I will just shoot him."

I protested, "Well, wait a minute." And I just eased over and slipped my rope around his neck. Dale came over and was going to help me tie him up and take him home. But when that sucker got up pretty close to me, he just laid his head over on the ground.

Puzzled, Dale asked, "What's the matter with that thing? Is he sick?"

"I don't know," I replied.

When I turned his head over, it was as limber as a rag. I looked at his eyes and exclaimed,

"He's dead! That's what the matter with him! I guess he had a heart attack when those dogs caught him. I don't what happened to him, but one thing's for sure, he's dead."

"Well, at least we won't have to pack him in," Dale sighed.

After skinning out the lion, we rolled up the skin and put it behind my saddle. By this time, it was getting dark again. We hadn't had anything to eat, you might say, in two days. The dogs hadn't eaten either. So we cut off the hind legs and front quarters of the lion and built a big fire up against the bluffs where we could scrape out the snow. We built up the fire in order to get the ground and the rocks warm so that we could bed down between the fire and the bluff. After fixing a place to sleep, we roasted the lion and gave it to the dogs, who ate most of it. I took a bite or two, and it wasn't too bad. In fact, it might have tasted good if I hadn't known it was a lion.

The next morning, we were tired, the dogs were tired, and we were about forty miles from home. As we rode, we had to fight a lot of snow, so when the dogs jumped a trail, we called them off because we couldn't afford to run them any farther. They were just about exhausted anyway and got to where they mostly just followed us along.

We rode all day and were still on the west side of the mountain trying to get to the east side. The snow was deep in the divide anywhere that we hit it. The closer we got to the divide, the deeper the snow. Then we ran into a logging trail that led down into some foothills.

"Dale, somebody's cutting logs up here!" I ventured.

"They sure are!" He agreed.

I suggested, "Let's follow the trail up the mountain and see where it leads us since it is kind of going in our direction anyway."

About two miles up the mountain, we ran into a camp.

"Hi, fellows!" Some old boy greeted us. "Get down and have something to eat."

I was already off my horse when I said, "We sure will!"

Dale threw a block of hay apiece to all of our horses.

Then we sat down and ate two pounds of cheese and a loaf of bread while the logger cooked some bacon and eggs and sourdough bread. Since it was getting dark again, and we decided that we had better head for home, which was still about ten miles away.

After going up the mountain some distance, Dale's horse finally gave out. He unsaddled him and turned him loose. Soon, my horse gave out also, and we released him. Then Dale put my saddle on Brutus, which I led up the mountain, trudging through heavy, knee-deep snow. Dale was following the dogs, which were behind me and the horse. He was complaining about his feet being cold. He thought they were frozen. Instead of boots, he was, as usual wearing shoes to make walking easier in case he needed to follow the dogs on foot during a hunt. I stopped and went back to check on him. His shoes were so hard that they seemed to be like solid steel. I climbed on up the hill and came upon a road that went over the mountain. I found an old bent-over yucca plant, kicked it over into the road, and set it afire. After Dale kind of thawed out his feet, he pulled off his shoes and socks, dried them out, and put them back on. With his feet warm, he could navigate again. We finally reached the top of the mountain with Dale riding Brutus, but he was so tired that I didn't know whether or not he was going to make it. When we started down the east side of the mountain, all the snow had melted there, but we were still seven miles from home. Riding double on Brutus all the way down the mountain, we got in about two o'clock in the morning, turned the horse loose and collapsed in bed where we stayed for about two days. We didn't do any hunting for a few days in order to let our horses and dogs rest. Then, too, we had to go back and get Dale's saddle and find the horses we left on the west side of the mountain.

Chapter 10
A Harrowing Catch

Then Dale and I decided to hunt on the north end of the mountains. With our dogs and horses, we camped right under Cochise's Head in a cave extending about fifty feet into the mountain. Even though the cave gets smaller toward the rear, we had plenty of room for ourselves, the dogs, and the horses. Also, people who had camped there before had covered the floor with pine needles to sleep on. The cave was warm. Water set just two feet inside the cave would not freeze. We stayed there one night.

The next morning we headed over the top of the mountain and down the other side where we set up our second camp where we had plenty of grass and water. We kept the horses in a cove hemmed in by our ropes stretched between two poles. After tying up the dogs, we went to bed. But about two o'clock in the morning the dogs started barking and raising cane. We hollered at them until they stopped barking and then went back to sleep. The next morning Dale was taking care of the dogs and horses while I started to cook breakfast. Dale walked up the trail a little way and hollered,

"Hey! You know something. I found what the dogs were barking at. It was a lion. Here's his tracks right here. He was coming down toward our fire last night."

We didn't even eat breakfast. We just turned the

dogs loose, figuring we would catch the lion in a few minutes. Boy! Were we surprised! I don't know where he went that night, but he certainly did some traveling. He went back up toward Cochise's Head and rimmed around some bluffs. We trailed that sucker until about one o'clock in the afternoon and then turned off the

Cochise's Head, taken from National Monument Park, Chiricahua Mountains.

mountain and went down the east side. The east side is where the feathers from Cochise's Head goes off through some rough, rocky, steep bluffs. It is a very steep mountain. Close to the bottom, we treed that lion. It was Dale's turn to climb the tree and flush out the lion. When Dale started climbing, the lion jumped right out. Soon we treed him again in a big old cottonwood. This time I went up the tree which had one limb extending way out over a dry, gravelly creek bed. The lion was out on a limb. I followed him out with a stick and loop in my rope, intending to slip the loop over his head. He just kept backing up and slapping at me. I asked Dale, "You got your rope?"

"Yeah!"

"You had better get a loop built, cause this limb is going to bend down, and he's gonna fall out."

Dale stood down below ready to rope the lion when he fell. Pretty soon, the lion backed out too far and fell right in front of Dale. But when he threw his rope at the lion, the loop settled uselessly across the lion's back. Because the dogs were crowding him, the lion raced toward a creek and crawled under a rock ledge.

We tried to punch him out with a long stick, but the lion just growled and slapped the stick, refusing to budge. On top of this little ledge was a crack. I rolled a rock away and exposed a hole right over the lion about two feet below. I told Dale,

"There's a hole up here. I am going to try to gouge him out from here. So put a loop over the hole where he would come out, and we probably can catch him."

I started to punch him and punch him, but he wouldn't do anything. Dale got a big stick and punched the lion, but the old lion just grabbed the stick and hung on until his head came up through the hole. Then he would fall back. After that happened a couple of times, I said,

"Hold it, Dale. Wait a minute. Let me get a loop around this hole."

After placing the loop around the hole I said,

"Now, put your stick down in there and see if you can pull his head up through there."

The next time Dale pulled the lion's head through the hole I jerked the slack out of the loop. The lion fell back into the hole, but he had my rope around his neck. We weren't sure how we would get the lion out, but we tied up the dogs so they wouldn't get hurt if the lion came out fighting. I was tying up some dogs on one side and Dale was tying up dogs on the other side when

I suddenly heard my rope go zinnnng through that rock! That lion had bolted from his position dragging the rope and heading straight for Dale who was still tying up dogs. The knot at the end of my rope hung in a crack in the rock. Just as Dale turned around, the lion hit the end of the rope and spun around with his tail right in front of Dale! Astonished, Dale just grabbed the lion's tail and held on while I got the rope out of the rock. Having the lion strung out between us, we dragged him over to a big pine tree where we could control him. I tied his feet together with some pigging string. Next, I put a stick in his mouth, put a loop around it and tied his mouth shut. We decided to take him home.

Every once in a while, the dogs came up and nipped the lion, causing him to kick and squirm and spit and making him hard to carry. He weighed about 135 pounds. We were trying to carry him on a pole, which didn't work out because there was too much brush to carry him side by side. And we couldn't walk single file because the one behind was carrying most of the load. About half way up the mountain, Dale simply gave out, and I was hungry, not having had any breakfast that morning. Neither one of us was in good enough shape to carry the lion very far. I had seen some cows around there the evening before. So I said to Dale,

"If those cows are still over there, we are going to have some beef in a little bit."

I didn't feel like walking very far, but I took my rifle and started looking for the cows. Not finding any of them, we decided to leave the lion because we were too tired to carry him any farther.

At a small clearing with a pine tree, we untied the lion's feet, wrapped him around the tree, and then tied his feet together on the other side of the tree. I had an old buckskin coat that I pulled off my horse and tied to the lion's feet. Then we mounted our horses and went on back to camp. After cooking some biscuits, meat, and gravy, we slept a couple of hours. And then we caught some fresh horses, hobbled them on top of the mountain, and headed back to get the lion, which had gotten loose from the tree and scrambled off down the hill about seventy-five yards. Since he left a scuffy trail, he wasn't hard to find. We carried him out on top, went home, and called Ernest, who came around the mountain the other way so he could get in closer. He took the lion on home and put him in the lion house to be kept for future hunting with dudes.

CHAPTER 11
WINDMILLS AND WRANGLING

About three or four miles down the mouth of the canyon where we had camped out and got this lion was a ranch owned by Bert Morgan. I already knew him pretty well when I went to work for him. He was kind of a rodeo hand. He taught me a lot about handling cattle, how to ride bucking horses, and a little of everything else. I never liked to ride bucking horses, but knowing how to do it came in mighty handy when I got to running with some of those big cattle outfits. When you went to work for one of them, you might as well figure that you were going to get some bucking horses right from the start because everybody else had already picked the good ones. Whenever one guy got fired or quit, his horses would be split up among the other cowboys who would trade what they didn't want for something they did want. Therefore, the first horses I got usually were a bunch of nuts. So working for Bert, I got to be pretty good at riding bucking horses. His horses didn't buck all that hard since they were just ponies, but it gave me an incentive to ride them even if they did buck.

I also built a lot of fence for Bert, but we had another excursion that year that was a little different from some of the rest of them. About a mile from San Simon were some professional people from California—doctors, lawyers, people who had a lot money they wanted to invest in a drilling operation. Apparently, they were looking for oil and were using a derrick about fifty feet high. But after drilling about five thousand feet they hit artesian water, which was under so much pressure that it blew the tools right out of the hole and tore the derrick all to pieces. They finally got the well capped, but not before they flooded the streets of San Simon. The water was very good and not the least bit salty, but I never did find out what they did with it.

It was still summertime when I went to work for Charlie Gardner. He was a good guy to work for, but I never knew what Charlie might do if he got mad. I heard that many years later, his temper got him into some really big trouble.

Charlie had quite a number of cattle in the San Simon Valley. Mostly, I worked on a big windmill with a sixteen-foot wooden wheel. I had climbed up through a hole in the platform right under the wheel to redo some of the wooden slats in the wheel when I spotted a sand devil, which is a strong whirlwind that can send sand miles high into the sky. They come up when the weather is really still and the sun is hot. This thing wasn't more than a hundred yards away when I spotted it. It was traveling fast and heading straight toward me. I didn't have time to turn the wheel around and get back down through the hole in the platform, and I knew that as soon as the sand devil hit, that the windmill was going to spin around and sling me off into the desert some place. I couldn't stay on the platform, and I couldn't get to the hole. So I grabbed the storm fan in one hand and the tail fan in the other and pulled them together to keep the wheel from turning. When the sand devil hit, it spun me, the wheel, and the fans round and round for about thirty seconds. But it seemed more like thirty minutes.

When I started with Charlie, he had a bunch of cows that he had dehorned and branded, mostly yearlings. It was the wrong time of the year for this kind of operation. Since the weather was hot, all the cattle had worms in their heads. He had a hospital crew on hand and had set aside a hospital pasture where he could keep all the bad ones. Some would get too sick to eat and Charlie would soak cottonseed cake and try to shove it down their throats with an ax handle. That didn't work. We set up tripods where we could hang the cows and try to get their legs to function, but that didn't work either. So Charlie took a pole ax and knocked any animal in the head that couldn't get up when he kicked it. Then he loaded them onto a flat bed truck and dumped them into the Aurora River where they either rotted or washed away.

One day Charlie's son went down to a windmill located on a section of land owned by the King brothers, who had a ranch up north of us. The windmill supplied Charlie's cattle as well as the cattle for the King brothers. But when Charlie's son got to the windmill, he found two guys had fenced in the windmill and were keeping Charlie's cattle from water. Old Charlie was mad as hell! He went down there with a gun intending to kill somebody, but all he found was an old man who said he didn't know anything about what happened.

So Charlie said, "Well, if that's the way you guys are going to do, you just keep that section of land up there."

Charlie owned about eight or ten sections of land around the windmill, but he didn't have any other source of water for his cattle.

Some time later, Charlie told me to build a fence around their section. One segment of the fence ran three miles. I couldn't find the metal government marker at the end where the fence was supposed to stop, so I used a compass and started digging postholes with the help of two other men. After we got the first strand of wire strung, we found the marker about fifteen feet away. I thought that was close enough, considering how rough the country was.

But Charlie's cattle couldn't last very long in that hot weather without water, so we jacked up a rear wheel on Charlie's truck and rigged up a system for drilling a well, and we hit water at about thirty-five feet. Then we built a platform and put a pump jack on it. By the next morning we had water running into a pond which we had dug with the help of two little mules. Later, we put up a metal tank and took pieces from four old windmills to make one good one. After we set the tower in concrete and mounted the windmill motor on top of the tower, we had everything ready except for hooking up the storm fans. I had put up the storm fan, but the tail fan was held up from a rod off the top of the head of the windmill. Well, Charlie was sitting on top of this head and holding the rod in place. He gave me the other end and told me to hook it into the tail fan. All I had to do was push it in place. Well, it was right in the middle of the day, the sun was shining, and there wasn't any wind. I had been looking up into the sun so much that I couldn't see very well anyway. I kept trying to reach out far enough to hook up the rod. When I looked down, I thought the platform on which I was standing extended farther out that it did. But what I was looking at was the shadow of the platform just below me on the ground. Thinking I had plenty of room, I stepped off into nothing and went straight down into a pile of sand. I landed on my feet and just stood straight up.

Charlie looked down and said, "What in the hell are

you doing?"

"I'm a gittin' down," I replied.

He said, "By gosh, I've been doing this all wrong. All this time I have been using the ladder."

Climbing back up, I got the tail rod in place, and Charlie's water problems were over.

After I finished my work with Charlie Gardner, I moved around quite a bit. A fellow who had bunch of horses on Charlie Gardner's place hired me to drive his horses to Deming, New Mexico, a trip of about one hundred miles. I stayed there and worked for him a long time until he went broke. Then I worked quite a while for the Flying U, another good outfit to work for. They had a lot of rough horses, rough cowboys, and rough country to work in.

Then I got a job building fence on a new highway to Hot Springs, now known as Truth or Consequences. As I was working on this fence, an old boy came by one day from the Ladner Ranch and said to me,

"You look like a cow puncher to me."

"Well, that's what I do best."

So I went to work for the Ladner's. Talking about rough horses, rough cattle, and rough country, that was the roughest outfit I ever worked for in my life. They had some tough cowboys and brush hands, but they were good people. The bunkhouse was like a hotel with eight or ten rooms down the side of it. Mounted over the doors to the rooms were heads from wild steers they had gathered out of the mountains. And there were a lot of wild cattle in the mountains that they never got out during the year and a half that I worked there. I never before saw such running cattle. I guess they were just born and bred like that.

The ranch had two little white mules, which they used to wrangle horses. That's all these mules were ever used for. The old boy that broke these mules trained them to go wherever the horses were. And when he got on one of the mules, he whipped him over and under until they found the horses. Since they were trained that way, nobody could hold one back once they were out of the corral. They'd go! They would buck for about the first fifty yards, and then they would throw up their heads, and all a rider could do was hang on and fight brush. You couldn't hold one until he found the horses, and then you could handle him as well as a horse. At four o'clock in the morning with frost or snow on the ground, it's hard to locate horses, especially if there is no moonlight. But those mules knew right where they were. They could smell them and go right to them.

The first time I wrangled horses, I sure had myself a ball! I hated to wrangle horses before daylight, but that was the ranch's custom. We had to eat our breakfast, saddle up our horses, and to be ready to go before daybreak. Sometimes we left before daybreak, depending on how far we had to go. That's the time of day when it is easiest to see cattle, just at daylight. After that, they start bunching up. In the middle of the day, cattle will lie down under a tree or something, making them hard to find.

One day I was revving around in some of the roughest country they had, and instead of riding a horse, I saddled up a mule named Lysol because a mule is sure footed like a mountain goat. They can go anywhere. I rode around in the bluffs and scared out a few cattle. I didn't drive them any place, but shoved them out into lower country. This dang mule was raised back north of that ranch about twenty-five miles, and every time he got a chance, he would go there.

I was riding this mule off a steep mountain going alongside a fallen pine tree. I guess a limb from the tree gouged the mule in the side, and he started bucking right beside the tree. Well, as he went up, there was an old dead limb that caught my chaps belt and just hung me up there. The mule just went on bucking down the hill. To get loose from there, I had to unbuckle my chaps. Then I pulled off my chaps and spurs. Of course, that mule headed for the north country, starting up a canyon. I rimmed around, carrying my chaps and spurs so I could travel. I just kept rimming farther and farther, and pushed him off the mountain into a box canyon. I didn't know it was a box canyon when he went in there, but it was. I finally hemmed him up and caught him. For a while I thought I was going to have a very long walk back to the ranch.

A big lake sat right on top of these mountains. In the wintertime, it practically froze solid. An icehouse had been constructed out of logs and lined with sheet iron. A second wall had been built around the house, with dirt packed between the two walls. Blocks of ice were cut from the lake during the wintertime to fill up the house. Then in the summertime, pack mules would bring down the ice in heavy canvas sacks to the ranch house. This icehouse was unique to the Ladners. None of the other ranches where I worked had a big cooler and a ready supply of ice to keep their produce fresh.

Dud Lee and friends
Branding Cattle

CHAPTER 12
SUCCESSFUL DECEPTION

After spending a summer working for Bert Morgan and Charlie Gardner, I went back to hunting lions for another year. We had several animals in the lion house which, we had caught over a period of weeks when I teamed up with Vince, Clell, and Dale to take Roy Hitchcock and his party from Rochester, New York, on a lion hunt. Younger people today don't recognize the Hitchcock name, but in those days the Hitchcock brand of belts and suspenders were nationally known for their high quality.

Roy showed up with a movie camera, the first I ever saw. I don't know how much of our expedition he filmed, but his main purpose was to shoot a lion. We hunted for days without seeing so much as a sign of a lion. Fortunately, Roy and his two companions were congenial and interesting conversationalists. We had guaranteed them a lion, and they just accepted the long hunt as part of the deal, while enjoying their ride through the open country.

One night at camp, Clell came over to me and confided,

"Listen, we gotta do something. We gotta get a lion for these fellows. I'm going over to Paradise and get one of our caged lions."

Dale and I stayed and took care of the dudes while

he drove to Paradise in his old car, returning about midnight when Dale and I helped him hide the lion among some trees away from camp.

The next morning Vince cooked breakfast while Dale and I wrangled the horses. Once the horses were saddled, we slipped off and pulled the trigger on the lion cage and then carefully watched which way he went.

Finishing breakfast, we mounted our horses for the day's hunt. Vince took the lead saying,

"I think we will go this way today."

We rode until we crossed a flat place in the trail left by the lion. About that time the big scout dog got a scent of the lion and bawled. Vince spoke up,

"Heck, there's been a lion right through here."

Dismounting, he put his palm down in the dirt and made some toes on it. Then he excitedly exclaimed,

"Here's a lion track!"

Moving on he said,

"Here's another one!"

"And another one!"

The dudes didn't catch on because they didn't know a lion track from a mule track. We tracked the lion for half an hour and treed him where Roy shot him. And so we maintained our reputation of always guaranteeing a lion to our hunters.

But the Lee brothers learned the hard way that hunting with dudes requires a greater awareness of safety. When Ernest started taking dudes on lion hunts, a fellow named Guy Mayer went along. He worked in Bisbee, and had been around the Lee brothers for years. In fact, he taught Clell, Dale, and Arthur how to shoot. They were all just kids when he was grown man.

On this particular lion hunt, the party was made up of Ernest, Vince, Clell, Dale, and Guy. They treed a lion right up against a bluff. Roy shot at the lion and barely nipped him but caused him to jump out over a bluff and run down the hill.

Guy was way back up on the hill about fifty feet on the other side of a tree from where Arthur was standing. When the lion went over the bank, Arthur ran down to the edge of the bluff and squatted down on his heels trying to see where the lion was going. Guy raised up to take his second shot at the lion, which he thought was on the edge of the cliff, but had already gone. He shot Arthur right through the heart. Arthur just raised up and threw his rifle out in front of him and said,

"Guy, you shot me!"

And then he fell dead. That's all he ever said, and he knew who shot him. Of course, that made it pretty rough for the rest of the boys. They had to pack Arthur

Arthur's tombstone, Paradise Cemetery.

on a horse about ten miles before they could get to a road.

Ernest didn't say much. None of them said too much because they were all good friends of Guy. But Ernest probably expressed the feeling of all the brothers when he said,

"Guy, if that boy had suffered a minute, I would have killed you."

It was just one of those tragic things that everybody had to live with.

CHAPTER 13
DEALING WITH DUDES

Ernest gave Dale and me the job of looking after Dick Borrel from Rochester, New York, where he worked for Bausch and Lomb Binocular Company. His wife was sole owner of French's Mustard. She gave us $400 a month to keep Dick with us. We didn't have to hunt with him. She just told us more or less to take care of him because she didn't want to fool with him while she spent some time in Tucson where she rented a suite of rooms doing whatever she did.

I got along well with Dick, but he would make Dale angry when he got up every morning by asking him,

"What's new?"

Dale would say,

"Dad dang it! You have been out as much as I have! You oughta know what's new."

We could be camped out for two weeks, and old Dick would needle Dale by saying,

"What's new?"

And Dale would flare up,

"Dad dang it! You know as much about what's going on as I do. I can't tell you what's new. Don't know nothing new!"

Dick got acquainted with a man and wife who ran a little store in Rodeo. The woman kinda flirted with old Dick once in a while. He liked that and called her the

"Desert Queen." He thought she was something else. She was a big woman, but pretty. Late one afternoon when Dale and I were at the Paradise Post Office, Dick said to Dale,

"Take me to Rodeo. I want to go see the Desert Queen."

Dale fumed,

"To heck with you! I ain't taking you nowhere. You can go hunting with us in the morning. We gotta get out early in the morning."

Dick argued,

"I don't want to go hunting in the morning. I want to see the Desert Queen. I want to go to Rodeo."

"I'm not taking you to Rodeo," Dale insisted, and stalked off down to the corral.

Then old Dick started in on me,

"Take me to Rodeo."

I protested,

"I can't take you to Rodeo. I haven't got anything to go to Rodeo for, and I don't know anything you got to go to Rodeo for. So I don't think we will go to Rodeo."

We argued for about ten minutes. Finally, he said,

"I'll tell you what I'll do. I'll give you twenty dollars to take me to Rodeo."

Brightening, I conceded, "Let's go to Rodeo!"

"Yeah, you handsome son-of-a bitch! I thought that'd get you!"

So we went to Rodeo. The trip didn't amount to anything, but he got to go to Rodeo.

Old Dick was as freehearted as he could be. At this time coats made out of thin leather patches were in style. The patches were all different colors but sewed together into one piece and then made into a coat. They cost about twenty dollars apiece, expensive at that time. Old Dick had a coat made for me, Dale, Ernest, the Desert

Queen—everybody. He also gave me the best set of binoculars I ever owned. Later on, I traded them for a car. He also bought me a .38 double-action pistol. Then he had a saddle shop make a scabbard and gun belt for me. Before he left, he gave everybody else something too.

Later, Dale and I were moving a bunch of horses prior to taking a guy named McKeel on a lion hunt up in the Black Mountains in the Black Range in New Mexico. We moved the horses up there so we would have plenty of mounts to use in hunting. While Dale was running these horses up the side of the mountain, he was wearing the pistol Dick gave me. The gun was bouncing and its butt was pinching Dale's butt on the side of the cantle of the saddle. He took off the gun, but instead of tying it to the front of the saddle where he could watch it, he tied it behind the saddle. While running the horses, he lost it. We searched all afternoon for it but never found it.

Anyway, Vince, Clell, Dale, and I started to hunt lions with McKeel, a very peculiar person from New Jersey. We hunted with him for two weeks without jumping any lions. Clell and Vince went back to Paradise to get a lion out of the lion house and brought him back to turn loose for McKeel to kill. He was happy to shoot his lion, but he wanted to stay on a while longer and hunt. Ernest agreed and left me at his request to stay with him. So the others left me with McKeel, four horses, and four dogs. Old Mac and I must have hunted for two or three weeks. We caught a bobcat or two and jumped a lion, but didn't get him.

Mac was kind of a crazy guy. He lay down by the fire one night wearing a whole bunch of clothes. He had on a coat with a wool jacket underneath. And under that, a wool shirt and a sweatshirt. But he had burned a hole in the back of the whole shebang about the size of a hat. Then he had on a heavy topcoat that didn't have hole in it. He wore these same clothes, day in and day out. I tried to get him to pull them off and throw them away and get some more. ,

"Naw," he said, "I'd rather have these."

He didn't care if they had holes in them. He would go to town looking that way.

He wanted me to go to South America with him, saying,

"I've got a plane which I will get up here whenever we get a little relief. And we'll go to South America, and boy, I'll show you one heckuva good time! We'll go back to New Jersey. You don't know what girls are until you go back there because there are ten girls there to one here. There are lots of girls, and I will introduce you around, and we'll have a ball. Won't cost you a nickel. You just come go with me."

But he was so crazy. I didn't want to get into that plane with him. I didn't know how well he could fly, or whether not he could fly at all. So I made excuses and never did go with him. I guess if I had, I would have gotten some where. I don't know where, but later Dale hunted with him in South America.

Chapter 14
A Little Luck, A Little Envy

Dale liked hunting so much that he would hunt twelve months out of the year if he could. In fact, years later he did hunt full time, not only in the United States, but also in Mexico and South America. He always wanted me to go with him, but some of the shots I made kinda got under his skin.

Once we set up camp in the Chiricahuas to hunt bobcats at night. We took about six dogs and started hunting about two o'clock in the morning. We usually ate breakfast around mid-morning. One morning we were coming back to camp, not having seen any bobcat tracks, when the dogs suddenly hit a trail and took off. We thought that if it were a bobcat, we would have him in a matter of minutes. The dogs ran about a mile and started barking treed. I said,

"Well, we got one."

We got one all right, but it wasn't a bobcat.

What we had was a four hundred pound bear in the top of a big spruce tree. It was against the law to kill a bear unless it was a stock eater. Dale said,

"Let's shoot him anyway."

"O.K.," I agreed. "Go ahead."

He had an old .25 .20 rifle and I had a German Luger pistol. Those were the only guns we had. The bear was about half way up the tree and we were trying to get a clear shot through the foliage. Dale shot, and the bear started climbing higher. I fired at him twice with the Luger and saw the hair part where I hit him in the side, but the shot didn't really hurt him. The bear climbed to the top of the tree and we took turns shooting at him with the rifle. We shot him so much that he put his head behind the tree trunk where we couldn't see him. Moving up the side of the hill, I told Dale,

"Give me that rifle up here. You·go around to the other side of the tree and get a stick and point it toward him and make him hide from you, and I will just stand here with the gun braced against a tree so I can get bead on him when he moves my way." Sure enough, when Dale pointed the stick at the bear, he moved around to my side of the tree. I shot. I didn't know where I hit him, but he came tumbling down out of the tree, breaking off limbs as he fell. He fell about sixty feet with the limbs breaking his fall and landed right on his butt. He just rocked up on his feet and down the hill he went, right by Dale, who, along with the dogs, took off after him.

They went down to the mouth of a little canyon and then turned into this canyon. Since I was up on the hill, I just cut across over a steep ridge so I wouldn't waste time going down the hill and then back up. With my rifle in my hand, I was climbing on all fours. Hearing a noise as I reached the top, I stopped and was surprised to see this bear coming right at me from the other side of the hill. I had to jump out of his way, but the bear didn't even look at me. He had been shot so many times that I wasn't anything to him. He just ran right by me and on down hill a ways and into a small cave. Dale and the dogs came over, and we tried to punch him out with a stick. He would grab the stick and let us pull his head out before turning the stick loose. I got on top of the cave and told Dale,

"Pull his head out there again, and I'll see if I can shoot him. Maybe we can get him out of there."

Dale pulled his head out, and I put the gun right down the back of his head and pulled the trigger and killed him. We dragged that sucker out of there and skinned him. He had thirty-eight bullet holes in him. His hide wasn't worth two cents, but we took the hide down to Paradise.

We stayed there over night and returned the next day to do some more bob cat hunting. Back on top of the mountain the next day, we went off in another direction over Hoovie and Rock Creeks. As the dogs went over a ridge, they picked up a trail and away they went. In a little bit, we could see what they were after. It was another bear. He would go up to the top of the ridge on one side and then he'd turn around and come back down the canyon. Then he would go back up again and then down again. He kept doing this with the dogs in hot pursuit. Dale and I were running our horses to death trying to keep up. So we just stopped at the bottom of the canyon. Finally, the dogs put him up a tree next to some bluffs about fifty feet high. We were riding up to the top of the bluffs when Dale said,

"If we get on top of those bluffs, we'll be about eye high to him, and maybe we can get that sucker."

After dismounting at the top of the bluffs, Dale lay on his belly looking at that bear with his .25 .20 trained on the bear. I was sitting beside him on my heels and said,

"Now Dale, you'd better kill him with that first shot because he's coming out of there. If you don't kill him, I'm going to shoot him with this Luger."

He didn't say anything, and pretty soon, he shot. A bear doesn't run down a tree headfirst. He comes down backwards. So here he came backing down out of that tree just a buzzing. I was holding this Luger in my hand over my head. I dropped it down as the bear passed, and pulled trigger. He turned all holds loose and fell out of the tree. About that time, I heard somebody up on top of the mountain.

"Yahoo!"

"Dad dang," said Dale. "You go down and see about the bear, and I'll go up there and see who it is and turn them the other way."

It turned out to be Carol Barfield, a kid we knew from Paradise. It didn't matter to him. He wasn't going to say anything to anybody about it. When I looked that danged bear over, he had one shot in him, right behind the ear where I hit him with my Luger. Dale was pretty miffed because he didn't like for me to outdo him in anything.

On another occasion, he had an old horse called Sidewinder who was corral spoiled. We could hardly get him into the pen. He would go right up to the corral gate with all the rest of the horses as if he was gonna lead them all in. But he would stop and look back until all the other horses got in. Then he would whirl and run like the devil. We'd have to run him, and sometimes we could get him, and sometimes we couldn't. Usually the best way to get him was to wait until he got up to the gate with all the other horses behind him, and then just crowd them all in at once. That way, the others would take him in with them. On this particular day, he didn't go into the corral, and Dale had wanted to ride him the next day. Because he had always been so difficult to pen, he had threatened to kill him before and use him for dog food. He wasn't the best horse anyhow. Now, with his patience at an end, he said,

"I'm gonna kill that sucker!"

Out in the horse pasture was a round knoll with a fence on two sides, and the corral was back on the other side toward the barn. The horse would just run around and around that knoll to keep from going into the corral. Dale hid in a ditch with his .30 .30 and waited while I chased the horse around that knoll toward him. As the horse came around, he shot and missed. So I ran the horse around a second time. Again, he shot and missed.

J.W. (Dud) Lee, taken in 1937, El Paso, Texas.

"Darn!" I fumed. "Gimme that gun and you go run him around."

It was getting dark and hard to see. If we were going to kill the horse, we couldn't waste any more time. So I hid in the ditch while he ran the horse around. Since the horse had been shot at twice, he didn't come by the ditch but turned and galloped up toward the top of the knoll. He was about a hundred and fifty yards away and running as fast as he could. I raised up out of the ditch where I rested on my elbows and just shot at the big part of the horse. I expected to hit him some place in the chest, knowing that he could still run two hundred yards after being shot. But when my bullet hit him, he stiffened all four legs in mid-air and just splattered to the ground.

I started walking toward him, and Dale came around to meet me. I knew from the way the horse fell that I must have hit him in the head because he wasn't moving at all, just lying dead still. Dale asked,

"Where did you hit him?"

"I don't know. I shot at his head." I lied.

The bullet had gone in under the horse's ear and tore off half the side of his head where the bullet came out on the other side. Dale responded the same way that he did when I shot the bear in the head. He didn't say anything for a little bit, but finally grudgingly ventured,

"You're gonna shoot at something's head some time and miss it."

Some of the rabbit shooting we did turned out the same way. Along with some other fellows, we were shooting rabbits for dog food. Dale was using a .22 rifle. I didn't have a gun with me. We came upon a rabbit just sitting still under a bush. Often rabbits won't move if they think they can't be seen. Dale shot and shot and missed. Another boy in the car shot and missed too. The rabbit then just hopped a little ways into some brush and out of sight. So I said to Dale,

"Gimme the gun."

I walked down to where I last saw the rabbit in some thick sagebrush. You could hardly see the rabbit running sideways through the brush. Now and then you could get a glimpse of it. The rabbit jumped up to run, but from where I was standing, he was going right down the trail straight away from me. He might as well have been sitting still. I shot, and down he came. Of course, from the vantage point of the other guys, he was running sideways, and they thought that was the dangest shot they ever saw. But Dale never said a word.

CHAPTER 15
SUMMER TRAPPING

Clell and Dale left Paradise to locate a mare to breed to a big Arabian stallion owned by a man named Barney. Consequently, I was alone one June day when Ernest got a call from Forrest Maulkins on the other side of the mountain claiming that he had found a lion track.

"I can show you the lion track when you get here. I got it covered up."

Ernest cautioned me,

"I don't know whether you are going to do any good or not, but if I were you, I would take some traps and see if you can trap him because it is too hot to run him."

So I took some traps and rode over to old Forrest's place. I tied up my horse down by the barn and came up to the back door at the same time his wife, a big fat woman, came out of the house, carrying a large pan of clabber to feed her chickens. Startled upon seeing me, she jumped and missed a big rock they used for a doorstep. She fell, dumping the whole pan of clabber on herself. To me, that was funny, but I couldn't afford to laugh until I got away. But after that, I always called her "Clabber." She was a good-natured old gal and took it in stride.

I stayed all night with Forrest and went to look at his lion track the next morning, which turned out to be a cow track that he was looking at sideways.

"You see here," I instructed, "Those are hoof prints. You are not looking at it the right way for a lion. A lion wouldn't make that kind of track."

When he understood, I continued,

"I'm going to see what I can do anyway. I might be able to trap a lion over here."

I went to the top of a ridge that looked like a good place where lions would come down for a passageway if they were hunting for something. Every time I saw a sign of a lion, I set a trap, baiting it with catnip. I spent that night with Forrest, too. When I checked my traps the next morning, a lion had tripped my second trap, which had a drag on it designed to hang up in some brush. But the lion, being too big and rambunctious, had broken the chain, which was big enough to hold most animals. I had three dogs that could track the lion, and I could track him since he was leaving a heavy trail with the trap on his leg.

I tailed him until about two o'clock when the dogs just quit because it was so hot. They were just lying in the shade panting and puffing from exhaustion. So I told Forrest,

"Take these dogs back home. I'm going to Paradise and get some more dogs to catch that devil."

Arriving at Paradise, I told Ernest what I had done. He approved,

"Well, take Skip, our best dog, and Freckles, and Buck back with you. And Vince is back home now. So take him with you."

Vince and I took the three dogs and picked up the trail where we had stopped the day before. We ran and ran that lion. Then he turned back into Cochise's Head and ran some more. We could see the marks where the trap was hitting the ground. This country in Cochise's

Head is too rough to even ride a horse through it. Today, this area is part of a national monument. In fact, I was present when the monument was dedicated to this famous Apache chief. It happened one day when Vince came home early and suggested,

"Let's go over to Cochise."

"What's over there?" I asked.

"They put up a monument and they are dedicating it today."

"Well, we've got time, so let's go."

When we arrived, a big celebration was already in progress. A crowd of about 150 people, most of whom I did not know, were listening to some dignitaries making speeches about the old days when Cochise was running wild in the Chiricahuas where we hunted most of the time. The dedication was near a mountain peak that was shaped like the head of Cochise. People who attended that day signed their names on slips of paper which were then locked in a tomb that was supposed to be opened in one hundred years. I guess in year 2030 another celebration will take place there when the names of those of us in attendance will be read.

Dismounting, I left my horse with Vince and Forrest and went on foot with the dogs, which had the lion cornered in some rocks. The dogs were baying, and the lion was just sitting there slapping at them to keep them away from him. Before I reached him, I could hear him banging that trap against the rocks. A flat rock about fifteen feet across lay above and adjacent to the lion. I climbed six feet to get on top of the rock. As I emerged on top on one side, the lion jumped up on top on the other side! The dogs were all around barking. The lion looked at me. Then he looked back at the dogs. I had a bead on the lion and was squeezing the trigger when old Skip bounded up the hill on the other side, right in my line of fire. I raised the muzzle of the rifle just as the shell exploded. If I hadn't, I would have killed one of our best dogs.

Hearing the shot, the lion jumped off the rock and was chased by the dogs about fifty yards to a big, high bluff. He wasn't going to jump off that bluff because it was too high. Besides, he was in no condition to jump with that trap hanging on him. I eased down to within thirty feet of the lion, which was sitting sideways to me. I drew a bead on him and shot him right in the side of the head, knocking him off the bluff.

Meanwhile, the dogs were barking treed, and Vince knew we had him. Old Forrest excitedly asked Vince,

"You think I can get in there? You think I can get in there? I'd like to get to where I can see him! I'd like to be there when he shoots him!"

Vince said,

"I don't know whether you can or not."

About that time, he heard my shot and said,

"Nope. No way. You're through."

We skinned out the lion and made our way back home.

Chapter 16
Trouble Spots

It was never my custom to look for trouble with anybody, but a few times along the way, trouble found me. When I was working for the Circle Dots, I had a camp way back on the backside of the Hueco Mountains, where I seldom, if ever, saw anybody. As I was coming into camp one day, I spotted a calf among some trees, but didn't see any cows with him. I wondered what the heck that calf was doing there in the trees by himself. When I rode up to him, I saw the reason. He was tied to a tree. I immediately suspected who had done this, but couldn't be certain. I didn't even get any closer, but turned off and went on to the ranch house. I got something to eat and changed horses. Just as it got dark, I headed back to the calf and took up a good surveillance point with a pair of field glasses. I sat there until one o'clock in the morning, but nobody ever showed up. I know now that the man who tied up the calf didn't come back because he had seen me. Finally, I took the rope off the calf, coiled it up, and put it on my saddle. Two or three days later, I was by his place. He had a homestead of fifty to seventy-five acres and broke horses. I rode up to his corral where he had a bunch of horses and was looking them over. I saw him looking at his rope on my saddle, but he didn't claim the rope. He didn't mention the rope at all. But he told another guy farther down toward the Texas border that he was going to kill me, saying,

"I'm going to kill that son-of-a-bitch."

"Well, we'll just have to wait and see, won't we?" I replied.

I carried a .45 automatic in my chaps, which had a pocket just like a scabbard. The handle of the gun stuck out so that I could bring it out shooting. And I was pretty good with a pistol. I became a good shot with a pistol when I was punching cattle near Ft. Bliss, Texas. The soldiers there used to come out on the ranch and look for Indian diggings, which were scattered around the area. I knew where all of them were located and passed this information on to the soldiers. They took a liking to me, and when they found out I had a .45 automatic they kept me in bullets since the army also used .45s. When they went out for target practice, they would have a lot of ammunition left over, and they would bring it to me in a gallon bucket. I used up boxes and boxes of that stuff. I shot at anything that moved. A rabbit could jump up as I was riding along, and I would whip out that old gun and shoot it without the horse even breaking stride.

So a few weeks after I was told that this man was going to kill me, I was riding back on the side of the ranch near his place. I saw him building a fence. I thought I would go by there and see if he still wanted to kill me. When I got within seventy-five yards of him, he turned his right side toward me. He had an old single action .45 on his hip and had it tied down to his leg. Oh, he was tough looking. I just rode right up to him, pulled off my glove, and stuck it in my chaps. Then I reached down and pulled the hammer back on my automatic and sat there with my hand on the gun, waiting for him to make a move. During the fifteen minutes that we talked, he never mentioned his gun nor made any move toward it. Rather than call his hand, I decided just to leave. I didn't see any use in agitating him since all I had was hearsay anyway. But I didn't ride straight away from him lest he shoot me in the back. I rode off a short distance at a forty-five degree angle, and then turned and rode at a forty-five degree angle the other way so that I could watch him all the time I was leaving. That was the last time I ever had any trouble with him. And any time I ever saw him after that, he didn't have a gun.

Later, when I was riding for the Boquillas Cattle Company, I sometimes went to rodeos around the country. A couple of other old boys and I went to a rodeo in Benson and stayed there three days. Of course, we just visited, drank beer, and had a good time like everybody else. The last night we were there, I was getting tired and sleepy from drinking more beer than I wanted. I wasn't drunk. I just didn't want any more beer. These other two guys were sitting over in a booth with a couple of girls. Since they were having a ball, I was more or less waiting for them so we could all go back home together.

I was standing with my back to the bar. I wasn't bothering anybody or talking to anybody when this old boy came walking by me, looked me over, and said,

"Well, hello you Texas son-of-a-bitch!"

I had my elbows on the bar, and he was standing about two feet from me. I just let my left arm slip off that bar. My fist caught him right on the chin, and he went under a table.

He got up sputtering apologies through a busted lip, "I was just joking! I was just joking!"

My eyes were as cold as my words, "You don't joke to me like that. I don't take those kinds of jokes."

But then I accepted his additional apology and forgot it. Naturally, all this broke up their little set-to they had going over there in the booth. After the boys said goodbye to the girls, we went down to the stockyards, got our horses and took off for the ranch.

On another occasion, Clell and I were at a dance when a guy came in who had had too much to drink. He announced,

"I can whip anybody in this town!"

That quieted everybody down, but nobody said anything. So he said,

"I can whip any son-of-a-bitch in this county!"

Still, nobody paid much attention to him, but Clell was getting a little restless about this time. Then the man said,

"I can whip anybody in this state!"

He turned just in time to see Clell, who had been running across the slick dance floor, sliding toward him. Clell hit him awfully hard and the guy hit the floor. When he finally staggered to his feet, he admitted,

"I just covered too damn much territory."

CHAPTER 17
STAMPEDE

One fall when I was working for the Circle Dots, the cattle were fat and in good shape and ready to be rounded up when a fellow with two horses offered them to Earl Bodine and me for extra mounts. Earl said, "Lee, you take the brown one and I'll take the black long-faced one."

Earl already knew about the brown one. He had tried to ride him before and had gotten thrown off five times. So I made a hackamore that didn't fit the horse very well and got ready to ride him. Everybody else was already saddled up and ready to go.

When I left the ground, the horse left the ground. I kicked at my right stirrup and missed, so I spurred him in the neck every time he jumped. Oh, he was hard to ride! That was the buckingest horse I ever rode. He bucked for a hundred yards. He'd go up high and kick out to one side and then kick out to the other side on the next jump. But I never did give him any slack. I just kept spurring him all that morning.

Sometime later, I had him in a corral, intending to fix the hackamore where it would fit better and give me better control, but I didn't get it fixed. And when he came out of that corral, he ran out like he was going to buck some more. I sank my spurs in as hard as I could, and he went to running. He headed up the mountain covered with very large, slick rocks. Since he was bare footed, I expected him to fall any minute. I couldn't do anything with him, so I just let him run. He went up the mountain, over the top, and down the other side, which was somewhat brushy. And I spurred the hell out of him. Of course, that made him run faster, but he never tried to buck any more. At the bottom of the mountain was an arroyo about four feet deep and six feet wide. I thought, right here is where we're going to wreck. Seeing the arroyo coming up, I loosened up in the saddle, so that if he went into that arroyo, I was going to get out on the other side. But when he approached the arroyo, he just lengthened his stride a little bit and kept going. He went about another half a mile before I got him stopped.

I met up with the guy in the bed wagon and said,

"I'm going to get me a fresh horse. I can't handle this one well enough to get any work done."

So I caught one of my horses and turned that one loose and never did ride him any more. But he would have made one helluva good horse if anybody had stuck with him because I had already spurred the bucking out of him. And when I spurred a horse, he knew he had been spurred because I always wore a pair of spurs I picked up in Mexico that had a large rowel with long spokes that had a pleasant ring when I walked.

The next day, we had gathered all the cattle from the east side of the Hueco Mountains and brought them to a string of lakes. We gathered a whole bunch more from that area and were then going to pick up all the rest from there back up to the main ranch house. We had about two thousand head of cattle. It was cloudy and a little bit rainy, but not bad. However, something spooked those cattle and they took off. I had been in little stampedes before, but this was my only big one.

When the cattle started running, I was riding point on the left side, and Doug Clayton, the boss's son, was riding point on the right side. Doug swung way out around the herd and came up on my side to help me turn the herd as I headed to the front. Together we turned the cattle and just kept pushing them and spinning them around. Soon the lead cattle were running into the drags in the back so that the entire herd was going around and around. Since the lead cattle couldn't run, they just stood there with their heads up while the other cattle milled around them, running at full speed. Doug and I went upon a little ridge and watched the stampede, which was beautiful. These were red cattle with white faces. So the center of the herd looked white while the rest was red, like a giant bull's eye.

They finally ran themselves out and stopped. Then we lined them out and took them home.

CHAPTER 18
RIDING AND ROPING

After I left the Circle Dots Ranch, they sold out and Reuben and I went to work for the Jeffrey boys at Datil, New Mexico. In the meantime, Dad had quit making whiskey, so we didn't have any more to sell. Reuben and I were punching cows, and Dad was doing the cooking. This was a time when we really enjoyed being together.

Dad was eager to see me ride because he had had some scrapes of his own in his younger days. He had worked for the XIT in the Texas Panhandle when he was about twenty years old. When he asked for a job, the boss said,

"Yeah, we can use you. There's an old dun horse out there in the corral. Go out there and saddle him up and go drive up some horses, and we'll get you a mount out of them."

Dad roped the old horse, which was gentle enough while he put the bridle and saddle on him. But when he hit the saddle, the old horse turned on him and bucked more than any horse he had ever ridden. When Dad landed on the ground, he thought,

"Well, if I am going to work here, I may as well learn to ride."

When he got back on the horse, he got bucked off again. By this time he was pretty disgusted with the horse, but went back a third time and started to get on. But the old man that ran the place had been standing there looking through the fence and said,

"Son, don't bother trying to ride that horse. You can't ride him. I just wanted to see how good a cowboy you were. Just leave him alone. We'll get you a mount after a while. Pull the saddle off him and turn him loose."

He worked for the XIT four or five months after that. During that time a colored boy came walking up. He had on his chaps, a rope strapped to his belt, and a little leather quirt snapped just under one leg of his chaps. When he asked for a job, he was told to go ride that same dun horse. He was told he could just keep that horse for his mount. This fellow just pitched a rope around the horse's neck—didn't even bother with a bridle or saddle. He just jumped on him and rode him bareback. The horse broke in two and bucked like he always did, but the fellow just sat on him and spurred him until he quit bucking. Then he herded cattle all afternoon with just a loop around that horse's neck. When Dad left the XIT, the guy was still on the job.

I rode for the Jeffrey boys most of that summer. Although it was too hot to hunt lions, two of them jumped out from under some bluffs one day. An old boy that was with me had a dog, and we chased one of the lions all over the country until I finally gave out. We lost him down in a creek anyway.

One day when we went out to gather some cattle out of the mountains, I was given a little horse to ride that wouldn't weigh over six hundred pounds. One of the cows was pretty bad. Riding with me was Bill Jeffrey who said,

"I want to catch that old cow because I am going to dehorn her right here because she is so mean. We'll get her out later, if we can. We hemmed her up against some bluffs, and as she ran by me, I threw a rope on her. She was going down hill. Man, she just took my little horse with her! He had all four feet sticking out forward, but it didn't do any good. She was dragging him on down. Finally, she went over an old pine tree that had fallen down. The tree stuck up about three feet high. The cow pulled my horse down until his front feet plowed under that tree, and that's where he stopped her. Bill went around that tree and caught her hind feet. We stretched her out, dehorned her, and then headed back down the canyon after we turned her loose.

Usually, it was my job to rope a cow by her hind feet because I was one of the best. I got that way working with Weldon Leach for the Bouquillas Cattle Company. We both loved to rope, and he was an expert at roping a cow's front feet. We had two good roping horses. Sometimes when we got back to the ranch about four o'clock in the afternoon, we would unsaddle the horses we had been riding all day and saddle up these two roping horses just to practice roping. One time when we had to brand a bunch of calves, one of the owners roped a calf and then let it run until someone threw it down. After watching this a while, I said,

"That's not the way to get the job done."

He said, "Can you rope them by their hind feet."

"I sure can."

"Then do it."

So I roped one hundred and ninety-six calves by their hind feet and never missed a loop.

But my obsession with roping got me into a messy situation when I was riding alone one day along the San Pedro River. I found an old wild cow and decided to rope her just to stretch my rope. The horse I was riding was pretty sorry and would run away from me if he had a chance. When I roped the cow, the horse wouldn't hold her, so I took a couple of turns around a tree. This cow was as wild as a Brahma bull and tried to gore me when I got off the horse to tie her feet. Finally, I just slacked off the rope and turned the cow loose. Then I was dodging her from side to side behind the tree to keep her from hooking me. Suddenly, the horse took up the slack in the rope on the other side of the tree. The rope hit me about the knees and knocked me face down in some wet caliche there by the river. The mud was so sticky that for a moment I couldn't see anything. Fortunately, no one was around to witness my embarrassment.

At summer's end, I went to see a friend of mine in the hardware business in Las Vegas, New Mexico. I had worked for him before he had sold his ranch at Deming. After a week in Las Vegas, I landed a job with an old guy who had a large ranch. He had a big house with a big garden and an orchard just below the barn.

Back in the spring, he had bought eight hundred head of steers. Now, he wanted to gather them in and ship them to market. This job lasted quite a while because he had a total of about two thousand head of cattle.

He also had a daughter about eighteen years old who had several of her girl friends visiting from Albuquerque, or from places where she had gone to school. She had a Shetland pony that was a mean little devil, but he was a lot of fun for these kids. They rode him bareback, and he wouldn't buck, but if they did something he didn't like, he would just reach around and catch their pants leg in his mouth and pull them off. They would get on one side, and he would pull them off on the other side. He wouldn't hurt the kids, but he wouldn't let them ride either.

I didn't care much for the wagon boss for this spread.

Humorless, he acted like he was better than most people were, and to make it worse, there was a great deal about cattle that he didn't know.

One day, we had gathered three hundred head of steers in the rain when the creek had risen high enough to swim a small cow. Crossing the creek, we had to keep our feet up because the water rose above the stirrups. This wagon boss was trying to run these cattle across the creek by just pushing them off in there. As fast as we got them up to the creek, they would run back. I dang near ran my horse down. Angrily, I said,

"Let me get up here and drag one of these cows across this thing. That'll get them started, and then the rest will go."

"Naw, hell," he said, "You can't do that. The cattle ain't gonna do that. You gotta push 'em in there."

Defiantly, I yelled,

"You're not gonna get 'em across that way!"

So I just roped a cow, got her up pretty close to me, and took off across the creek. With other men pushing from behind and me leading that old cow across, the rest of the cattle kind of fell in behind her and all of them went on across the creek.

The fact that I knew how to get the cattle across the creek and the wagon boss didn't know how made him so mad that he wouldn't even speak to me for three or four days.

CHAPTER 19
WILD HORSES

At the foot of the mountains a few miles from Paradise, lies a little place called Round Valley where wild horses roamed free, led by a little brown mare sensitive to the least noise or scent. She could get wind of me a half mile away, and when she bolted, the whole herd followed. I wanted to pick out a few horses to break and ride, but trying to cut out a horse from the herd was futile since the mare was so easily spooked. They could get away by running up and down the canyons and wear out my horse in the chase.

One day when Clell and Dale were gone, I happened to ride through the bottom of a brushy canyon at Round Valley. The bottom of the canyon was covered in small gravel, making it easier on my horse than going along the hillsides. Glancing up, I saw that brown mare on a ridge with the herd of horses. I decided to just kill the mare in hope of getting close enough to the herd to get me some horses. Dismounting, I led my horse through the brush to within two hundred yards of the mare where she was standing broadside to me on a ridge. I aimed my .30 .30 a little high, expecting the bullet to drop some. But it didn't drop enough.

At the sound of the shot, that horse didn't jump. She didn't run. She didn't do anything. Rather, she just turned around and started walking, and all the other horses milled around her. Some acted as if they wanted to run but stayed with the mare, which just kept walking. I couldn't figure out what happened to her.

Remounting my horse, I rode toward them, but she still didn't run. So I got behind the herd and drove all the horses over a hill, along a ridge, and down a slope to a corral we had just over the hill from Paradise. Amazed, I drove them right into the corral. After I got them penned up, I found out what was wrong with the mare. My bullet had creased her right across the top of the withers, that meaty part where the mane grows. I shot right through that. Now I had heard of creasing horses so they wouldn't run, but I had never done it before. I had even forgotten that horses could be creased, and now I had accidentally creased one. This really didn't hurt the horse. When she healed, she was as wild as ever.

When Clell and Dale came home, we picked out a few good horses and turned out the rest. One of mine was a sorrel stocking-legged horse, which I called Angel. Although a good horse, he was mean to kick.

One day Dale rode Angel when the two of us went to Bill Lee's place to move some cattle. Bill was Dale's brother. On the way back, Dale got off Angel to open a gate through which we needed to pass. He led the horse through the gate, but his mind was somewhere else because he didn't turn Angel around. He just walked back by the side of the horse to shut the gate. A cattle guard lay right beside the gate. Just as Dale closed the gate and turned around, Angel caught him on the thighs with both hind feet and sailed him right over the cattle guard. Because he had been standing so close to the horse, he wasn't hurt. Getting up he said,

"Well, I don't know what I want to do with this danged old horse a-kickin' so."

I put in my two cents,

"Well, if he did me that way, I'd kick the belly off that son-of-a-gun."

Dale didn't know how to do a lot of things, and that was one of them. So he got the reins in one hand and the saddle horn in the other hand while standing on the ground. Dale kicked him in the belly. When he did, the horse whirled around, kicked at Dale, jerked loose, and kept going. I went after the horse and brought him back. Dale said,

"I don't know how to do that. You show me."

I got off my horse. Taking Angel's reins, I grabbed the saddle horn and put my left foot in the stirrup. Having a good hold on the horse, I kicked him twice in the belly. He whirled and started jumping and finally reared up on his hind feet and swung me around in front of him. I turned the saddle horn loose and ended up standing in front of him as he pawed at me with both front feet. I ducked to keep him from hitting me in the head. As I did, he hit me between the shoulder blades with the heel of his foot and tore my shirt plumb down to the belt, skinning my back.

I didn't know what else to do, so we decided to teach Angel a lesson some other time. When we got to Paradise, I told Dale,

"I'm gonna hunt something to put on my back."

"I got something here," he replied.

We went into the kitchen where he pulled something off a shelf. I didn't pay any attention to what it was and already had my shirt off. He poured a handful of Watkins Liniment on my back and rubbed it in. Lord! I never was so near on fire in all my life. I cussed him out but couldn't do anything else.

We never needed to teach Angel a lesson. That was the last time he ever kicked. I rode him to Ernest Lee's house one day and tied him up a short distance from the house. A little later, I looked toward the horse and was dismayed to see a little three-year-old girl hugging Angel's hind legs. Afraid that I would spook the horse if I intervened, I breathlessly watched until the girl walked away from the horse, who seemed to sense that a harmless child was near him.

Angel turned out to be a fine mount, being equally good at punching cattle or hunting lions. And when he let me use him as a packhorse to carry lions, I knew that a bond of trust had been established between us.

CHAPTER 20
BREAKING HORSES

One time when Dale and I were breaking horses, I was riding a little blue horse while his was a big sorrel. We weren't having much trouble with them. I had ridden him the day before, but once in a while he would still buck with me. I had a type of saddle that isn't seen much any more. In place of having a D ring for the cinches, it had a B ring so that I could move the cinches away from the front legs of the horse. Well, I had been riding him as a double rig, and the cinches behind his legs had rubbed a sore spot, causing the leg to bleed. So I just moved the cinches back and didn't cinch him up too tight because he was hurting there.

We were heading out to gather some cattle for Bill Lee, who was getting ready to ship them to market. It was kinda cold with frost on the ground, so after we got about two hundred yards from the barn, Dale said,

"Let's lope a ways."

"O.K.," I said.

We hit a lope, and that horse I was riding bowed his neck and started jumping. On the second jump, he skinned right out of the saddle. I hit the ground in front of him while still sitting in the saddle with my feet in the stirrups and holding the reins. The horse stood there looking over my shoulder.

Dale laughed and laughed. He turned around and

headed back to the barn.

"Where in the hell are you going?" I asked.

I must have made a big impression on the ground, for he said,

"To get a shovel and dig up your picture."

"Well, maybe you had just as well go ahead."

But he didn't. I saddled up my horse again and rode him pretty well after that. However, he did do some beautiful bucking at times.

Once we were moving some cattle and had made a drive across a big open flat with Clell to the east of me and Dale to the west of me. I was bringing up the middle when I ran out to drive a cow back down the hill. That old horse broke in two with me! And he could really buck. He kept me riding my very best. I wasn't the best at riding bucking horses, but I was good. He bucked all the way down a grassy slope into a little canyon. When he hit bottom, I pulled him up. He turned and bucked right back up the canyon. I got him pulled up again. Disgusted with him, I jerked him around and headed him back down the hill a ways toward an arroyo. He trotted a few steps, and then bowed his neck and started bucking again. He turned out of this arroyo and bucked back up the hill. Of course, he couldn't buck much going up the hill because it was too steep. But he went under a mesquite tree and caught the saddle horn on a limb about the size of my leg. He kept bucking until he broke the mesquite limb which was caught on the saddle horn and hanging on his neck. I just let him buck because it didn't bother me much with the limb hanging on to him.

When Clell saw the horse going down into the canyon, he thought he had fallen with me. He came loping over that way, and when he got there, the horse was still bucking with the limb on his head. Clell stopped him and pulled his head up so he could remove the limb. So after we gathered some cattle and put them into a corral, Dale, who had seen some of what had happened, said,

"Heck, I can ride that horse."

Clell interjected, "Dale, I don't think you can."

"I know dang well I can."

"Well, why don't you get on him and try it?"

"O.K., I'll ride him with Dud's saddle and let the stirrups out."

So we pulled off the saddle to let out the stirrups to fit Dale and then put the saddle back on the horse. Dale got on him.

The horse didn't even wait to be turned around. He just bowed his neck and went to bucking. On the third jump, he put Dale ten feet into the air. He came down with flailing arms and legs, looking like an octopus. Dale gave up and Clell said,

"I told you that you couldn't ride that horse."

I reset the stirrups to fit my legs and rode the horse back to the ranch house. Apparently, he was bucked out for the day. Later, I worked on the Red River Ranch at Springerville, New Mexico, for about a month before I got a job at Clayton, New Mexico, breaking horses. I arrived in Clayton late in the day at a hotel where cattlemen hung out. Walking out on the street, I approached a big, tall ugly looking guy about six feet four, who was wearing boots and spurs,

"Fellow, do you know where a cowboy can go to work?"

He didn't even turn around, just stood there looking across the street. Since he apparently ignored me, I turned away and took about three steps when he asked,

"What can you do?"

"I can do anything from breaking horses to fixing

windmills."

"You can break horses?"

"Yeah."

"Where are you staying?"

"Right here in this hotel."

"I'll pick you up in the morning, and we will go out and look at the horses."

"I don't need to look at the horses. We can just go there. I can handle horses."

"Nah, I want you to look at them."

He came by the next morning before daylight while I was still in bed. Arriving at the ranch, he showed me fifteen pretty three-year-old quarter horses and offered me so much a head to break them. I agreed, and he put me up in an old sheep camp that was a good place to break horses. A creek with a big sand bar on it ran right by the house. The sand, being pretty deep, was a good place to run horses because neither the horses nor I would get hurt in a fall. But the gate on the other side opened right up to a mountain side topped by a flat mesa, about three-quarters of a mile up. The whole side of the mountain was covered with rocks, cactus, yucca, soap weeds, and century plants, all with sharp spines. I could turn a horse through there and keep him so busy looking where he was going that he didn't have time to buck. I got off to a bad start. That first evening after we got the horses in the corral, he said,

"I'll help you catch one, and we'll stake him out there to a log."

"We just as well take the prettiest one first," I replied. He was a dark sorrel with a flaxy mane and tail. I picked up both his front feet, laid him down and put a hackamore on him. This corral had been used to pen up sheep and was covered with sheep droppings hard as marbles. When we turned the horse loose, he jumped up and skidded on those sheep droppings and fell with his right leg sticking straight out from his body.

"Well," he said, "I guess he's ruined."

"Looks like it broke him all to pieces, doesn't it? I never saw one do like that."

He concurred, "I never did either. Go ahead and turn him out. I'll come down in the morning and get rid of him."

But next morning that danged horse was gone! I rode to the top of the mesa and all around, but never did see him. But the boss finally found him and brought him back to the corral. Fortunately, the horse's injury wasn't permanent. He limped for a while. After he healed, I broke him, and he turned out to be a fine saddle horse.

I really enjoyed breaking these horses. Being such good-blooded horses, they didn't buck much. While riding one of these broncs through the rocks, I could really put the rein on him as he was picking a place to put his feet. When I wanted to turn him, if he wouldn't turn, I'd wait until we got to one of those old soap weeds and pull his head right into the spines. After that whenever I wanted to turn the horse, he'd suck up the bits and turn. I could really put a rein on him because he would pay attention.

I broke one of the best cutting horses I ever saw. At first, I had a lot of trouble with him. To break the horses, I always put them in a squeezer chute to make it easier to put a hackamore on them. Late in the afternoon, I put this horse in the squeezer chute, intending to put a hackamore on him and stake him out to a log all night, so that he would be ready to lead the next morning and not give me any trouble. That's the way I broke horses to lead. But he reared up and fell over backwards in that squeezer chute. There wasn't any way he could turn over and get back upon his feet. I worked and worked. I roped him and tried to pull him over with another horse. I tried pulling him out of the chute. Nothing worked. I went to the headquarters of the ranch about three miles away and told the boss,

"I need somebody to help me get a horse out of the squeezer that's in there on his back."

He said, "I'll go down there with you, and we'll take the chute apart."

We took the bolts out of the bottom of the chute, and took one side apart to let the horse out. Finally, I got him staked out. And he turned out to be one heckuva fine horse.

When I finished breaking those horses, I called a guy on the old Swift Ranch in Hugo, Colorado, for whom I had gathered cattle the previous fall when he was shipping cattle. He said that he needed some help and invited me to go to work for him. That was a big mistake. I hated that job. The ranch was about seventy miles east of Denver in the wide, open spaces where there were no trees, no bushes—just sagebrush and bear grass and not much of that. But snow was a foot deep. Naturally, the cattle had to be fed since there was no grazing. I would put about a ton of cottonseed cake on a cart pulled by mules or big horses. Tied behind the cart a big tire formed a drag to clear a path for the cottonseed cake. After clearing a path, I would turn the mules around, and they would follow the cleared path while I scattered cottonseed cake on the ground. You would think the cattle would miss a lot of it, but they ate nearly all I put out. Doing this daily in the cold winter snow for so many cattle got to be a terrible chore.

Snow fences crisscrossed the ranch, and high board fences were built near stack lots containing hay. Four or five hundred head of cattle could be fed behind each of these fences. But in a blizzard, the cattle on the outside kept crowding in close to get out of the wind, causing many cattle closest to the fence to be trampled to death. During one particular blizzard, we had all the cattle in corrals or behind snow fences except fourteen head of two-year-old bulls. They were in a pasture covering about five square miles. Through the blowing wind and freezing cold, I rode and rode looking for them. Clumps of bear grass accumulated snow, making humps all over the pasture. Then I noticed a place that looked like four or five of those bear grass humps stacked up in one. But these humps were not bear grass. Every one of those danged bulls had lain down and gotten snowed in! They were warm under that snow and just lay there. I was mad because they hadn't come in with the other cattle and I had to ride in all that freezing weather. I roused them up to drive them back to the barn, but then they wanted to run and play in the snow, making it difficult for me to drive them in. But I got them to the barn, and the boss was happy. That was the main thing.

When the weather warmed up, I saw a rattlesnake as I was riding along. It had always been a tradition for a cowboy to kill a rattlesnake because they bite cattle. Most of the time they don't kill the cattle, but they make them sick for a long time. I got off my horse, doubled up my rope and rapped this snake two or three times and killed it. Then there was another one rattling beside me. When I turned to hit him with my rope, rattlers began to appear from everywhere. They were coming out of the ground faster than I could count them. I thought, "Man alive! This is no place for a poor boy!" So I got on my horse, hit a lope, and got out of there.

The warm weather also brought the grasshoppers. At first, they weren't big enough to fly, but they crawled, and everywhere they went, they mowed all the vegetation right down to the ground. We tried to kill them by putting poison on a manure spreader and put it in front of them as they traveled, but that was not very effective. The boss bought long rolls of metal flashing to make little fences leading to an open barrel of kerosene buried to ground level. The grasshoppers would follow the metal fence and drop right into the kerosene, which would kill them. However, that wasn't fast enough either. Then matters worsened when the grasshoppers began to fly. They could fly cross-country. Where they crawled across a road, cars running through them made a slick, mushy mess. By the time June arrived, I was fed up with snow, rattlesnakes, and grasshoppers. This was no place for a decent cowboy. I decided that if I ever got back to some cool running water and grass, I was gonna stay.

So I gathered up my outfit and headed south to Springerville, New Mexico. Reuben was there. He was working for Wade Phillips of Phillips 66 who owned the big Philmont Ranch. After staying with Reuben for a few days, I received a letter from Lyo saying that people were being hired to work in the mines at Bisbee. I was getting tired of running around and decided to give up the cowboy life for good. So I traded my saddle for a trailer in which to haul my stuff behind my old Pontiac and headed south for Bisbee. Two days after I arrived, I went back to work in the mines and stayed fourteen years.

EPILOGUE

DUD LEE

He left Bisbee and the Copper Queen Mine, which had been bought by Phelps Dodge by that time, and moved to Springfield, Missouri, in 1953. Here, he owned and operated several service stations until he retired in 1987. Presently, he lives with his wife Mary on ten acres where he raises calves near Billings, Missouri.

LYO LEE

He left the mines in 1941 to train horses and to start a racetrack at Ft. Wachuka. Horse racing introduced him to Roy Gill of Sasady, Arizona, who hired Lyo to train horses for him for many years. Lyo made history with Roy's famous Quarter Horse Barbara B when the four-year-old mare beat the Thoroughbred Fair Truckle by two-and-a-half lengths at Hollywood Park at Los Angeles in 1947. Millions of dollars changed hands on the race. The entire account is detailed in the August 6, 1947, issue of Southern Horseman. Lyo died in Florida on July 7, 1989.

CLELL LEE

Clell raced horses along with Lyo for a time when he had his own track. Later, he married a woman who owned a ranch at Alpine, Arizona, where he worked until he died of cancer in 1979.

Dale Lee

Dale became a full time professional hunter, not only in the Western United States but Mexico and South America as well. His biography is in a book entitled Life of the Greatest Guide by Robert McCurdy. He died in June 1987.

Tom Lee

Tom managed a ranch west of Springerville, New Mexico. He died of a heart attack in 1944.

Vincent Lee

Vincent became a full-time professional hunter in Arizona and New Mexico. He was killed when he broke his neck after being thrown from a mule while riding along the Mogollon Rim in Arizona in 1941.

Reuben Wright

Reuben worked on several ranches in New Mexico and the Texas Panhandle. He died of a heart attack shortly after the Lee reunion in Albuquerque, New Mexico, in 1978.

Rita Belle Greenlee Lee

After Dud's and Rita's divorce was final, she married Auther Wiley Reed in 1936. They owned and operated a farm near Ackerly, Texas. She died following surgery for a brain tumor in 1966. Auther died of complications from Alzheimer's disease in 1987.

Lyo Lee with his quarter horse,
Barbara Bee

ABOUT THE AUTHOR

James V. Lee was born December 10, 1926, to Rita Belle Greenlee and Judson Warren (Dud) Lee in the O.K. Community near O'Donnell in the Texas Panhandle. Besides O.K., he grew up in various locales in West Texas, New Mexico, and Arizona. When his mother remarried, he was finally able to call home a small farm west of Ackerly, Texas.

James was graduated from Abilene Christian College in 1949 with a Bachelor's Degree in English and earned his Master's Degree in Education from Southwest Texas State University. James married the former Hazel Juanita Lee (yes, same last name, no kin) in 1949. They have two married children, Kerry and Gail.

Starting with his service in the U.S. Navy, James has led a varied and interesting life as a successful salesman and educator. As a civilian teaching aboard U.S. Navy ships for five years, he traveled extensively in forty countries and "more islands than I can remember." His interests include traveling, writing, physical fitness, and gardening. James and Nita make their home in beautiful Central Texas.